Russia

Other Books of Related Interest:

Opposing Viewpoints Series

Culture Wars

Free Trade

Human Rights

At Issue Series

Does the World Hate the U.S.?

Should the U.S. Do Business with China?

U.S. Policy on Cuba

Current Controversies Series

Developing Nations

Illegal Immigration

"Congress shall make
no law . . . abridging
the freedom of speech,
or of the press."

First Amendment to the U.S. Constitution

The basic foundation of our democracy is the First Amendment guarantee of freedom of expression. The Opposing Viewpoints Series is dedicated to the concept of this basic freedom and the idea that it is more important to practice it than to enshrine it.

OPPOSING
VIEWPOINTS®
SERIES

Russia

Viqi Wagner, Book Editor

GREENHAVEN PRESS
A part of Gale, Cengage Learning

GALE
CENGAGE Learning™

Detroit • New York • San Francisco • New Haven, Conn • Waterville, Maine • London

Christine Nasso, *Publisher*
Elizabeth Des Chenes, *Managing Editor*

© 2009 Greenhaven Press, a part of Gale, Cengage Learning.

Gale and Greenhaven Press are registered trademarks used herein under license.

For more information, contact:
Greenhaven Press
27500 Drake Rd.
Farmington Hills, MI 48331-3535
Or you can visit our Internet site at gale.cengage.com

For product information and technology assistance, contact us at

Gale Customer Support, 1-800-877-4253
For permission to use material from this text or product, submit all requests online at
www.cengage.com/permissions

Further permissions questions can be emailed to permissionrequest@cengage.com

Articles in Greenhaven Press anthologies are often edited for length to meet page requirements. In addition, original titles of these works are changed to clearly present the main thesis and to explicitly indicate the author's opinion. Every effort is made to ensure that Greenhaven Press accurately reflects the original intent of the authors. Every effort has been made to trace the owners of copyrighted material.

Cover photographs reproduced by permission of © Pete Turner Stone Getty Images.

LIBRARY OF CONGRESS CATALOGING-IN-PUBLICATION DATA

Russia / Viqi Wagner, book editor.
　　p. cm. -- (Opposing viewpoints)
　　Includes bibliographical references and index.
　　ISBN-13: 978-0-7377-3767-7 (hardcover)
　　ISBN-13: 978-0-7377-3768-4 (pbk.)
　　1. Post-communism--Russia (Federation) 2. Russia (Federation)--Economic conditions. 3. Russia (Federation)--Social conditions--1991- 4. Russia (Federation)--Politics and government--1991- I. Wagner, Viqi, 1953-
　　DK510.76R858 2009
　　947.086--dc22
　　　　　　　　　　　　　　　　　　　　　　　　　　　　　　2008032034

Printed in the United States of America
1 2 3 4 5 6 7 12 11 10 09 08

Contents

Chapter 2: Is Russia Moving Toward Democracy?

Chapter 3: How Is Western Culture Influencing Russia?

Chapter 4: What Is Russia's Greatest Challenge?

Why Consider Opposing Viewpoints?

> *"The only way in which a human being can make some approach to knowing the whole of a subject is by hearing what can be said about it by persons of every variety of opinion and studying all modes in which it can be looked at by every character of mind. No wise man ever acquired his wisdom in any mode but this."*
>
> *John Stuart Mill*

In our media-intensive culture it is not difficult to find differing opinions. Thousands of newspapers and magazines and dozens of radio and television talk shows resound with differing points of view. The difficulty lies in deciding which opinion to agree with and which "experts" seem the most credible. The more inundated we become with differing opinions and claims, the more essential it is to hone critical reading and thinking skills to evaluate these ideas. Opposing Viewpoints books address this problem directly by presenting stimulating debates that can be used to enhance and teach these skills. The varied opinions contained in each book examine many different aspects of a single issue. While examining these conveniently edited opposing views, readers can develop critical thinking skills such as the ability to compare and contrast authors' credibility, facts, argumentation styles, use of persuasive techniques, and other stylistic tools. In short, the Opposing Viewpoints Series is an ideal way to attain the higher-level thinking and reading skills so essential in a culture of diverse and contradictory opinions.

In addition to providing a tool for critical thinking, Opposing Viewpoints books challenge readers to question their own strongly held opinions and assumptions. Most people form their opinions on the basis of upbringing, peer pressure, and personal, cultural, or professional bias. By reading carefully balanced opposing views, readers must directly confront new ideas as well as the opinions of those with whom they disagree. This is not to simplistically argue that everyone who reads opposing views will—or should—change his or her opinion. Instead, the series enhances readers' understanding of their own views by encouraging confrontation with opposing ideas. Careful examination of others' views can lead to the readers' understanding of the logical inconsistencies in their own opinions, perspective on why they hold an opinion, and the consideration of the possibility that their opinion requires further evaluation.

Evaluating Other Opinions

To ensure that this type of examination occurs, Opposing Viewpoints books present all types of opinions. Prominent spokespeople on different sides of each issue as well as well-known professionals from many disciplines challenge the reader. An additional goal of the series is to provide a forum for other, less known, or even unpopular viewpoints. The opinion of an ordinary person who has had to make the decision to cut off life support from a terminally ill relative, for example, may be just as valuable and provide just as much insight as a medical ethicist's professional opinion. The editors have two additional purposes in including these less known views. One, the editors encourage readers to respect others' opinions—even when not enhanced by professional credibility. It is only by reading or listening to and objectively evaluating others' ideas that one can determine whether they are worthy of consideration. Two, the inclusion of such viewpoints encourages the important critical thinking skill of objectively evaluating an author's credentials and bias. This evaluation will illuminate an author's reasons for taking a particular stance on an issue and will aid in readers' evaluation of the author's ideas.

It is our hope that these books will give readers a deeper understanding of the issues debated and an appreciation of the complexity of even seemingly simple issues when good and honest people disagree. This awareness is particularly important in a democratic society such as ours in which people enter into public debate to determine the common good. Those with whom one disagrees should not be regarded as enemies but rather as people whose views deserve careful examination and may shed light on one's own.

Thomas Jefferson once said that "difference of opinion leads to inquiry, and inquiry to truth." Jefferson, a broadly educated man, argued that "if a nation expects to be ignorant and free . . . it expects what never was and never will be." As individuals and as a nation, it is imperative that we consider the opinions of others and examine them with skill and discernment. The Opposing Viewpoints Series is intended to help readers achieve this goal.

David L. Bender and Bruno Leone,
Founders

Introduction

> "Vladimir Putin is not a democrat. Nor is he a czar like Alexander III, a paranoid like Stalin, or a religious nationalist like Dostoyevsky. But he is a little of all these—which is just what Russians seem to want."
>
> —Paul Starobin,
> Atlantic Monthly

In 2000, 30 percent of the Russian people lived below the poverty line. Russia's foreign debt was more than 100 percent of its gross domestic product and its economy was near the bottom of the list of world economies by size. Today Russia's economy is the ninth-largest in the world and is still growing by more than 7 percent per year. The treasury holds the third-largest gold and currency reserves in the world and the poverty rate has dropped to 15 percent. Any attempt to understand how that happened, or predict what will happen next, begins and ends with Vladimir Putin, president of Russia from 2000 to 2008 and a man *Time* magazine called "a critical linchpin of the 21st century" when it named him 2007 Person of the Year. In 2008, *after* Putin left office, he still ranked second on *Time*'s list of the world's 100 most influential people—a clear indication that though Russia has a new president, the Putin era is not over.

Putin was born in 1952 in Leningrad (now St. Petersburg) into a working-class family. At Leningrad State University he joined the Soviet Communist Party, and when he graduated with a law degree in 1975 he was recruited by the KGB, the combined security agency, intelligence agency, and secret police. With the fall of the Soviet Union in 1991, Putin resigned from the KGB and then rose through a series of political positions to acting prime minister of the Russian Federation under Russia's first post-Soviet president, Boris Yeltsin.

Yeltsin was a hero of the Russian independence movement whose popularity waned during his presidency, which was plagued by corruption, political and economic chaos, and the rise of a group of wealthy businessmen called "oligarchs." According to former Moscow bureau chief for *Business Week*, Paul Starobin, the oligarchs had "infiltrated Yeltsin's Kremlin, made fortunes in rigged privatization auctions, and seemed to regard the state as their private preserve." Putin, not yet a well-known politican, was campaigning for the presidency on a tough law-and-order platform when an ailing Yeltsin unexpectedly resigned at the end of 1999, vaulting Putin into office ahead of rival candidates. He was elected to a four-year term in 2000, enjoyed a record 83 percent public approval rating during his first term, and won reelection in 2004 by a 71 percent landslide vote.

Once in power, Putin moved quickly, some say ruthlessly, to resolve several crises. First he sent Russian troops into Chechnya, a province in the southwestern region of Russia called the Caucasus, a long-troubled area where an earlier guerrilla insurgency led by Islamic militants had just been revived (and was believed responsible for a rash of bombings in Moscow). In this so-called second Chechen war, Russian forces destroyed Grozny, the Chechen capital, and took control of most Chechen territory, where they still keep sporadic insurgent attacks in check.

Second, Putin pleased the Russian people by treating the oligarchs like gangsters and breaking their political hold. Some he arrested and charged with embezzling state property. Some he forced into exile. One, the billionnaire Mikhail Khodorovsky, who challenged Putin by bankrolling his political opposition, he jailed on fraud and tax evasion charges and turned his oil company, Yukos, over to the state. Western observers criticized Putin for disregarding the rule of law, but ordinary

Russians saw Putin cleaning house, and approved. The fact that he filled empty government posts with what are known as *siloviki* troubled the West, however. *Siloviki* are Russian politicians who were once KGB or Soviet military officers— they believe in a strong central government and military and in state ownership, and/or control of natural resources and the economy. They also want to restore Russia's "greatness" and Moscow's control of the former Soviet republics, and there is a xenophobic element in their views.

Third, when Russia was rocked by a terrible attack on a middle school in Beslan (a city about 40 miles from the Chechen border) by Islamic terrorists in 2004, in which some 330 hostages, mostly children, were killed and nearly 700 were injured, Putin responded by enacting a series of drastic anti-terrorism measures that bothered civil rights advocates but won him even more popular and *siloviki* support. Henceforth, regional governors required Kremlin approval. (The Kremlin is the seat of Russian government; the word is roughly analogous to "White House.") Controls over foreigners were tightened and lawmakers considered reinstating the death penalty for convicted terrorists.

Fourth, Putin presided over an amazing economic recovery. His role is debatable, but as Russia watcher Michael McFaul writes in a December 2007 *Slate* article, there is no doubt that during his presidency (and largely thanks to rising world oil prices) "real disposable income has increased by more than 10 percent a year; consumer spending has skyrocketed; unemployment has fallen from 12 percent to 6 percent. . . . Russians have never been richer. Public opinion polls show that this economic growth, after a decade of recession, makes Russians feel more stable and better off compared to the Yeltsin era."

Fifth, at least as important as Putin's domestic overhauls is Russia's invigorated presence in international politics. With a rebuilt military behind him, Putin negotiated arms deals with Syria and nuclear reactor deals with Iran. Russia enlisted

China, Iran, and four Central Asian republics to form the Shanghai Cooperation Organization, a military alliance and counterpart of the North Atlantic Treaty Organization, or NATO, of which Russia is not a member. Putin's political rhetoric toward the United States became more strident, his assertion of Russia's rightful place as a major player in foreign affairs more confident.

By 2006, though liberal critics said that Putin had become an autocrat and betrayed the democratic principles he was constitutionally bound to uphold, most Russians seemed either indifferent to or supportive of his methods and policies. Given the choice between order and freedom, most chose order. When Valentina Matvienko, the governor of St. Petersburg, was asked whether Russia would be better off as a parliamentary republic with no president, she replied, "We are not ready for such an experiment. The Russian mentality needs a baron, a czar, a president. . . . In one word, a boss."

The Russian constitution bars a president from serving more than two terms in succession, however, and despite 80 percent approval ratings, Putin promised he would not interfere with free elections in March 2008 to determine a new president. Not likely, said skeptics, who predicted that Putin would find a way to run the country behind the scenes. Events seemed to bear out this prediction: After a campaign often described as a foregone conclusion, Putin's loyal subordinate Dmitry Medvedev won the election and took office on May 7, 2008. The next day Medvedev appointed Putin prime minister of Russia. Putin had already accepted the position of head of Russia's biggest political party, United Russia, which holds a two-thirds majority in the legislature.

According to *Atlantic Monthly* correspondent Jeffrey Taylor in a July–August 2008 article, however, Putin's effort to handpick his replacement may backfire: "Not only does any form of power sharing run counter to the currents of Russian history, but Medvedev's electoral victory followed nasty factional struggles among those passed over by Putin." In other words, the *siloviki* are not happy.

The authors in *Opposing Viewpoints: Russia* debate Russia's current complicated situation in the following chapters: What Is Russia's Role in International Politics? Is Russia Moving Toward Democracy? How Is Western Culture Influencing Russia? and What Is Russia's Greatest Challenge? Their arguments suggest a variety of answers to the all-important question, "What happens next?"

OPPOSING
VIEWPOINTS®
SERIES

What Is Russia's Role in International Politics?

Chapter Preface

When the Cold War ended with the breakup of the Soviet Union in 1991, the world quickly looked to integrate the Soviet Union's main successor, Russia, into the Western community of states. Russian president Boris Yeltsin expressed his commitment to democratization and the transition to a Western-style market economy, and the process was soon underway. Beginning in 1994, the G7—the major industrialized democracies of the United States, United Kingdom, Canada, France, Germany, Italy, and Japan—became the G7 + 1, meeting separately with Russia after its annual summit to discuss global problems and issues of mutual concern. In 1997, Russia gained full member status and the group became the G8. In 2002, Russia gained a sort of partner status in the North Atlantic Treaty Organization (NATO), a military alliance based on a mutual defense treaty signed early in the Cold War by Western democracies that opposed the Soviet Union. The NATO-Russia Council formed in 2002 stopped short of admitting Russia as a member state but gave the country an important role in discussions of security issues.

But in recent years, integration has stalled over several contentious issues. NATO expanded its membership to include several central and eastern European former Communist countries over strong objections from Russian president Vladimir Putin, who viewed this as a violation of U.S. promises that NATO forces would not be stationed east of Germany. NATO also began planning a new missile defense system in Europe, which Putin also opposed as likely to spark a new arms race; in late 2007, when NATO wouldn't back down, Russia suspended an important arms limitation treaty, straining U.S.-Russia relations. The Russia-NATO relationship became even more frayed in May 2008, when Russia announced plans to station troops in breakaway regions of Georgia and opposed U.S. efforts to get Georgia and Ukraine admitted to NATO.

The growing tension reinforces the conviction of some U.S. policy makers and analysts that Russia remains an imperialist, antidemocratic country that should be isolated from the West.

Leonid Gozman, deputy chairman of the Russian political party Union of Right Forces, and Carnegie Endowment for International Peace associate Michael McFaul disagree with this view. They argue (in an article on the Carnegie Endowment for Peace's Web site) that full integration serves both Russian and Western interests, and plot this roadmap:

> To jumpstart the process of integration, G8 leaders ... should state unambiguously that they want to see Russia become a full-fledged member of *all* Western multilateral institutions. They should [spell out concrete milestones for] Russia joining NATO, ... even if the roadmap stretches twenty years long. ...
>
> European leaders must also outline a timeline and criteria for Russia's membership into the European Union. ... It is also necessary to fortify those multilateral institutions in which Russia is already a member—the United Nations, the OSCE [Organization for Security and Cooperation in Europe], the Council of Europe, Russia-NATO Council, and even the Shanghai Cooperation Organization. ... Russian membership into the World Trade Organization [is] long overdue.

If integration fails and Russia "drifts back toward state-led autarky," Gozman and McFaul insist, the West will lose a critical ally in the fight against global terrorism and nuclear proliferation. The viewpoints in the following chapter consider whether such a partnership is possible or whether Russia has already drifted too far toward authoritarianism and set out on a different, incompatible path.

> *"Instead of the Red Army, the penetrating forces of Russian power . . . are now Russian natural gas and . . . Russian electricity."*

Russia Is the World's Next Energy Superpower

Fiona Hill

In the following viewpoint, Fiona Hill argues that Russia is well on its way to regaining the superpower status once held by the Soviet Union, the communist confederation whose largest and most powerful member was Russia. However, Hill contrasts Soviet influence, which depended on military power, with Russia's present-day influence, based on its near monopoly on natural gas and electricity supplies in Eurasia. To its credit, Hill says, Russia is not pouring its profits into defense, as in the Soviet era. Instead, Russia is using its energy riches to create jobs and increase production of consumer goods, thus boosting trade, immigration, and regional stability. Fiona Hill is a fellow in the Foreign Policy Studies Program at the Brookings Institution, a progressive think tank in Washington, D.C.

As you read, consider the following questions:

1. What economic and cultural factors have made Russia a "migration magnet" for Eurasia, according to the author?

2. What are Gazprom and UES, and where have their markets expanded since the late 1990s, according to Hill?

3. What does Hill mean by "soft power?" In Hill's view, what should Russia do to increase its soft power?

In recent years, Russia has transformed itself from a defunct military—although still nuclear—superpower into a new energy superpower.

New Uses for Oil Revenues

Although Russia has retained many of the vestiges of Soviet "hard power"—including nuclear weapons and a massive conventional army—it is not the superpower of old. New energy revenues have not been used to boost military spending or to revive Russia's defense industry at the expense of every other sector as in the Soviet period. Oil wealth has been transformed more into butter than guns.

And there is more to Russia's attractiveness than oil riches. Consider the persistence of the Russian language as a regional lingua franca—the language of commerce, employment and education—for many of the states of the former Soviet Union.

Russian Pop Culture

Then there is a range of new Russian consumer products, a burgeoning popular culture spread through satellite TV, a growing film industry, rock music, Russian popular novels and the revival of the crowning achievements of the Russian artistic tradition.

They have all made Russia a more attractive state for populations in the region than it was in the 1990s. Over the last several years, Russia has become a migration magnet for Eurasia.

New Prospects

Millions of people have flooded into Moscow, St. Petersburg and other Russian cities—from the South Caucasus [the region between the Black Sea and the Caspian Sea] and Central Asia in particular—in search of work and a better life.

Instead of the Red Army [as the Soviet Union military was known during the Cold War], the penetrating forces of Russian power in Ukraine, the Caucasus and Central Asia are now Russian natural gas and the giant gas monopoly, Gazprom, as well as Russian electricity and the huge energy company, UES—and Russian culture and consumer goods.

Gazprom is the primary provider of gas to the Eurasian states and has regained its position in markets like [the former Soviet republic of] Georgia, where other companies had entered in the late 1990s. UES has similarly expanded its markets, especially in the Caucasus and Central Asia, where early energy sector privatizations brought in foreign investors.

Defining the Term

In addition, private firms—such as Russia's Wimm-Bill-Dann Foods—have begun to dominate regional markets for dairy products and fruit juices.

Russia may not be able to rival the United States in the nature and global extent of its "soft power"—which Harvard Professor Joseph Nye defines as emanating from three resources: "[a state's] culture (in places where it is attractive to others)," its political values (where it lives up to them at home and abroad) and "its foreign policies (where they are seen as legitimate and having moral authority)."

Regaining Influence

But Russia is well on its way to recovering the degree of soft power the USSR [Soviet Union] once enjoyed in its immediate sphere of influence.

Russia: In Control of the World's Energy Supply

Russia will soon exert such sway over the supply of oil and natural gas that the OPEC [Organization of Petroleum Exporting Countries] crisis of the mid-1970s could seem trivial. Its pipelines will flow east into Asia and west into Europe and tankers will sail from Siberia to California. Russia will soon have such control over energy supply and pricing that it will be able to do anything it wants politically. . . .

While the rulers of the Middle East have required simply that the West turned a blind eye to their domestic habits in return for a steady energy supply, the Russians are likely to demand a far steeper price. The cost of not developing realistic alternatives to oil and gas within a few years will be taking orders from Moscow.

Philip Delves Broughton,
"Beware Russia, Energy Superpower,"
First Post, October 12, 2006.
Copyright © First Post News Group Limited 2006.
Reproduced by permission.

Since 2000, Russia's greatest contribution to the security and stability of its vulnerable southern tier has not been through its military presence on bases, its troop deployments, or security pacts and arms sales.

Rather, it has been through absorbing the surplus labor of these states, providing markets for their goods, and transferring funds in the form of remittances (rather than foreign aid).

Central Asian states in particular are fearful of the social consequences of large numbers of labor migrants returning to the region from Russia if there were to be a political backlash against migrants or a Russian economic downturn. This migration to Russia has become a safety valve for the whole region.

More Powerful Than the United States?

As a matter of fact, Russia has the potential to achieve the economic and cultural predominance in Eurasia that the United States has in the Americas.

It will succeed in this mission if the influx of migrants to Russia continues, if Russian business investment grows in neighboring states, if regional youth continue to watch Russian TV and films, purchase Russian software, CDs and DVDs and other consumer products.

Trade—Not Military Muscle

Most of all, it would succeed if the heavy hand of Moscow is pulled back—and the hand of commerce is extended instead in Russian foreign policy.

Given this list of "ifs," clearly some skill is required to draw upon Russia's soft power resources in crafting a successful regional policy.

The current U.S. failure to capitalize on its own undisputed soft power and growing global anti-Americanism demonstrate the risks involved, and the limits of soft power if a state is not seen to live up to its own values abroad or its foreign policy motivations are questioned overseas.

It is by no means assured that Russia's increasing soft power will be used to positive effect. But the prospect is clearly there—and should be encouraging Russia's current leadership to chart a new regional policy for itself in Eurasia.

| "*Russia is indeed an energy colossus, but it is a giant with limited reach and standing on only one foot.*"

Russia Is Not the World's Next Energy Superpower

Carol R. Saivetz

In the following viewpoint, Carol R. Saivetz disputes the conventional wisdom that Russia's "vast [energy] resources make it a superpower to be reckoned with." In fact, Saivetz argues, Russia has been unable to get controlling stakes in pipeline networks that supply oil and gas to Europe and China, doesn't have the funds to maintain existing pipelines or build new ones, and consumes too much of its own energy production to make it anything but a regional exporter of energy. Carol R. Saivetz, a foreign policy expert, is a researcher at Harvard's Davis Center for Russian and Eurasian Studies and a visiting scholar at Massachusetts Institute of Technology's (MIT) Center for International Studies.

As you read, consider the following questions:

1. What is the size of Russia's natural gas reserves?

Carol R. Saivetz, "Russia: An Energy Superpower?" MIT Center for International Studies, December 2007. Copyright © 2008 MIT Center for International Studies. All rights reserved. Reproduced by permission.

2. What non-Russian options are European and Asian countries pursuing for their energy supplies?

3. Why does the author argue that Gazprom needs Europe as much as Europe needs Gazprom?

As Vladimir Putin nears the end of his second term [as of December 2007] as Russian president, it is clear that energy exports have become a major component of a resurgent Russia's foreign policy. According to the conventional wisdom, Russia's vast resources make it a superpower to be reckoned with. Not only is it a major supplier of natural gas to the states of the former Soviet Union, it also sells oil and natural gas to Europe and has made new contract commitments for both oil and gas to China. Additionally, as the January 2006 cutoff of gas to Ukraine, the January 2007 oil and gas cutoff to Belarus, and Gazprom's threat (again) to Ukraine in the wake of the September 2007 parliamentary elections indicate, Russia is willing to use its resources for political purposes.

The conventional wisdom continues that none of this is surprising. [Vladimir] Putin acceded to the Russian presidency [in 2000] resolved to restore Russia's superpower status and to use energy to that end. The Russian Federation's Energy Strategy, dated Aug. 28, 2003, formally states that Russia's natural resources should be a fundamental element in Moscow's diplomacy and that Russia's position in global energy markets should be strengthened.[1] In his own dissertation, Putin argued that the energy sector should be guided by the state and used to promote Russia's national interests.[2] And, the rector of the Mining Institute [where Putin received his advanced degree] and currently one of his energy advisors wrote: "In the specific circumstances the world finds itself in today, the most important resources are hydrocarbons. . . . They're the main instruments in our hands—particularly Putin's—and our strongest argument in geopolitics."[3]

Yet, the conventional wisdom is at best only partially accurate. When Putin and other Russian officials refer to Russia as an energy superpower, they seem to mean a country that possesses a bounty of energy and will use its resources to ensure Moscow's influence on the world's stage. In contrast, the true picture of Russia's energy resources and the attempted politicization of their uses is far more nuanced and complex. Russia's energy policies—resource and infrastructure development and its use of the energy weapon thus far—raise major questions about Russia's energy superpower status.

Energy Blackmail

The January 2006 cut-off of natural gas supplies to Ukraine made headlines. The reporting indicated that Russia was using energy to punish Kyiv for its 2004 Orange Revolution and that Gazprom, the state-owned natural gas company, wanted to gain control of Ukraine's pipeline infrastructure. Energy has been a contentious issue between Moscow and Kyiv since the Soviet collapse, but in December 2005, Gazprom escalated tensions when it demanded that Ukraine pay world market rates for its gas. The government in Kyiv asked for a phased-in rate hike, but Russia instead cut off gas to Ukraine, resulting in serious downstream disruptions. Under intense international pressure, a deal was quickly made: A shadowy intermediary, RusUkrEnergo, would purchase 17 billion cubic meters of gas from Gazprom, at $230 per thousand cubic meters, blend it with cheaper gas from Turkmenistan, and sell it at a guaranteed price of $95 per thousand cubic meters. Steady price increases have occurred since then.

The January 2007 stoppages to Belarus began with Gazprom demanding a steep price increase, with steady rises thereafter to world market rates; in addition, Gazprom demanded 50 percent ownership of Belarus's gas pipeline network. As for oil, Russia initiated export duties on oil sold to Belarus. (Prior to January 2007, Russian oil had been piped to Belarus duty free; however, Belarus garnered huge profits by selling refined products to Europe.) Belarus retaliated by charging Russia an export fee and reducing the amount of oil flowing to Poland. Russia then blocked all oil exports. Again under international pressure, oil flowed freely within days.

In both cases, Russia appeared to have made short term gains: most obviously, Gazprom won the price wars. Moreover, many claim that Russia seemingly influenced the outcome of the March 2006 Ukrainian parliamentary elections in which Viktor Yanukovich, the loser during the Orange Revolution, became prime minister. In Belarus, Minsk was forced to recognize Moscow's claim to a large share of the profits from the sale of refined products and to agree to a debt-for-equity swap of part of its pipeline system. What makes the Belarus case so interesting is that Moscow was clearly willing both to risk another disruption of supplies to Western Europe and to endure damage to its prestige in order to gain major control over Belarus.

Beyond the former Soviet states, the two crises highlighted European vulnerabilities to supply disruptions and raised the possibility that Russia might use its resources to influence European policies. Soviet/Russian supply to Europe began in the 1970s and has continued virtually without disruption until two years ago [2006]. Currently, 43 percent of European energy consumption is oil, while only 24 percent is gas. Yet, gas utilization will rise as Europe limits it use of coal. Christian Cleutinx, director of the EU[European Union]-Russia Energy Dialogue, estimates that the European Union's gas requirements will increase by 2020 to approximately 200 million metric tons/year. Of that, 75 percent will be imported, mostly from Russia.[4]

In addition to increasing its European market share, Gazprom has sought downstream infrastructure investment opportunities in Europe. Concerned, the European Union is looking both to limit the ability of non-EU companies to purchase distribution and refining assets in its territory and to force Russia/Gazprom to open [its] pipelines to outsiders. In an effort to enhance competitiveness, recent draft regulations mandate separating resources from transmission infrastructure. The proposed rules have strong implications for Gazprom, which could not own controlling stakes in distribution networks and would have to offer reciprocal access to its domestic pipelines. Press reports at the time of the EU announcement noted that Konstantin Kosachev, head of the Duma's [Russian parliament] International Affairs Committee, threatened to retaliate against foreign investors.[5] And most recently, Aleksandr Medvedev, the head of Gazprom Export, threatened that Europe risks a doubling of natural gas prices if it implements the new legislation.[6]

Even before the discussions about the proposed EU-wide policy, Gazprom executives threatened to shift export eastward toward China. Russia has already signed several deals with China and announced new pipeline projects to supply Beijing's growing market. Over the long-term, such a shift in emphasis is, of course, possible; however, effecting it in the short- to medium-term is inherently difficult.

Vladimir Milov, a Russian energy expert, notes that Russia's limited capacity and technology make it only a regional supplier of energy. He argues that the great distances and high construction costs hinder the development of pipeline infrastructure to China.[7] In fact, this past summer [in 2007], Russian officials announced considerable delays in new gas pipeline construction to China, and Moscow and Beijing have been unable to agree on oil prices or oil pipeline routing. Thus, at the present time, the threat to redirect exports is hollow.

How Much Does Russia Have?

Even if Russia were to increase energy, particularly gas, supplies to Europe and successfully complete new oil and gas in-

Major Recipients of Russian Natural Gas Exports, 2005

Rank	Country	Imports (BCF/Year)	Domestic NG Consumption
1	Germany	1,291	43%
2	Italy	824	30%
3	Turkey	630	65%
4	France	406	26%
5	Hungary	294	62%
6	Czech Republic	252	84%
7	Austria	246	70%
8	Poland	226	47%
9	Slovakia	226	108%
10	Finland	148	105%
11	Romania	140	23%
12	Former Yugoslavia	134	57%
13	Bulgaria	101	89%
14	Greece	85	96%
15	Switzerland	13	12%

Sales to Baltic and CIS States, 2005*

	Ukraine	2,113	79%
	Belarus	710	100%
	Baltic States	205	100%
	Azerbaijan	120	36%
	Georgia	46	100%

*Includes some re-exports of Central Asian gas.

TAKEN FROM: EIA, BP (2006), CIS and E. European Energy Databook, 2006.

frastructure to China, the question remains: Can Russia meet all of its export commitments? Most experts estimate that Russia has 60 billion barrels of proven oil reserves, largely located in western Siberia. In the initial post-Soviet period, oil production fell precipitously, but output has steadily increased—during 2005–2006, Russia became the second-largest producer of oil after Saudi Arabia. As exports have grown,

Russian domestic consumption of oil has declined. Recent data indicate that Russia exports approximately 4 million barrels per day; of that, almost 1.3 million barrels per day are piped through the Druzhba Pipeline, which traverses Belarus and Ukraine. Due to the multiple crises with these two former Soviet republics, Russia is currently building additional pipelines to bypass Belarus, Ukraine and the Baltic states, and is considering other projects that would eliminate the need to ship oil from Novorossiisk [on the Black Sea] through the Bosphorus to Europe. Despite these significant plans to increase export capacity, it is estimated that many mature fields are post-peak and that future production will grow at only between 1.5 to 2.5 percent, derived in large measure from new projects in Sakhalin.[8]

Russia holds the world's largest reserves of natural gas, approximately 1,680 trillion cubic feet, and it is also the largest exporter. Lacking liquefaction technology, Russia exports all of its natural gas through pressurized pipelines. Production has remained relatively flat overall, increasing by only 1 percent to 2 percent per year; moreover, Gazprom has invested little in new fields and its three largest fields, which produce 70 percent of output, have suffered annual decreased production.[9] Company officials are hopeful that new fields, such as the recently acquired stake in Sakhalin II and the Shtokman fields, will bolster production.

Thus far the discussion has not centered on domestic consumption and supplies, which are crucial factors in judging Russia's ability to meet its forward contracts. Currently, more than half of Russia's energy consumption is gas; however, domestic gas prices are effectively subsidized. The government acknowledges that prices will increase, but Putin has declared that even at peak they will equal no more than two-thirds of international prices. Low prices do not promote conservation: In 2006, experts estimated that by 2010 domestic gas consumption would rise by 24 billion cubic meters (bcm), or by 6 percent to 7 percent per year.[10] Herman Gref, minister of economic development, predicted likely domestic shortages of 5–6 bcm. In comments on Oct. 31, 2006, he noted that "Russia is encountering some real restrictions on economic growth due to a shortage of energy resources." These forecasts were seconded by ministry predictions that output would grow by only 0.9 percent in 2007 and 0.6 percent in 2008.[11]

Estimates vary regarding the extent of Gazprom's gas deficit, but most analysts agree that Gazprom will need both to develop new fields and import gas from Central Asia in order to meet its contractual obligations. With regard to new fields, the story of the Shtokman fields is illustrative. The fields hold 3.7 trillion cubic meters of gas, but the location north of the Arctic Circle renders them technologically challenging. A year ago, [in 2007], Gazprom withdrew the international tender for the fields, opting instead to develop them by itself. At the time, the decision seemed congruent with other actions to ensure state ownership of energy resources, but it also indicated that Gazprom had decided to rely on new pipelines instead of liquefaction technology. Gazprom apparently rethought its position and in July 2007 reopened the tender, ultimately awarding 25 percent to the French company Total and more recently an additional 24 percent to Norway's StatoilHydro. According to Russian press accounts, these new agreements represent open acknowledgment that Gazprom lacked the ability and technological know-how to develop the fields on its own.[12] It can also be seen as recognition that export via new pipelines, instead of in liquid form, would limit the market for the gas from Shtokman.

Russia has been aggressive in trying to lock up long-term Central Asian commitments—especially from Turkmenistan. For the moment, Russia and Gazprom control Turkmenistan's exports, mostly through Soviet era pipelines, and Turkmenistan will export about 2.1 million to 2.5 billion cubic feet to Gazprom in 2007.[13] In May 2007, it seemed that Gazprom and Russia had secured their goal: The new Turkmen president, Gurbanguly Berdymukhammedov, along with his Kazakh and Russian counterparts, announced a new gas pipeline along the Caspian coast to connect with the Gazprom grid. And in mid-October, at a Caspian Sea summit, Russia made a bid to limit the abilities of the other Caspian [coast] states to export via non-Russian pipelines.[14]

Gazprom's plan, however, may be delayed, if not thwarted, by the apparent determination of the new Turkmen government to explore export options. President Berdymukhammedov postponed until mid-December the final agreement for the Caspian coastal pipeline. The deal, championed personally by Putin, was signed only after Gazporm agreed to a thirty percent increase in the price it was willing to pay for Turkmen gas. Nevertheless, despite the new tripartite arrangement, other choices remain possible. Prior to the October 2007 Caspian summit in Teheran, the British minister of state for energy, Malcolm Wicks, traveled to Turkmenistan to explore new energy agreements and Berdymukhammedov visited the U.S. and held meetings with several Western energy company officials. The Turkmen president has announced renewed interest in the U.S.-proposed trans-Caspian gas pipeline, a project rejected by the mercurial late President Saparmurat Niyazov, and is moving forward on a deal with China for the construction of a pipeline east. Interviews in October in Ashgabat, the capital, suggest that the Turkmen government will announce a significant deal with a major Western energy company in the near future.[15] In mid-November, the *Times* of London leaked a report that the United Kingdom and Turkmenistan had signed what one official called a "protocol of intentions" to allow British companies to operate in the Turkmen energy sector.[16] Although the size of Turkmenistan's reserves is uncertain, it seems increasingly probable that there will be less gas available for Gazprom in the future.

Is Russia an Energy Superpower?

That Russia is destined to remain a major energy supplier to its immediate neighbors and to the rest of the world is not at issue. What is an issue, however, is whether Russia's resource development strategy is adequate to meet future demand. As argued, Russia has not invested in refurbishing gas infrastructure and seems to be relying on new finds such as Sakhalin and Shtokman to bolster supplies. Yet work on Shtokman has not begun. It is also clear that Turkmenistan is no longer willing to be a source of cheap gas for Gazprom.

There is also the question of whether the networks of supply will be solely commercial or whether these ties will be politicized. As states such as Armenia and Moldova have succumbed to Gazprom's pressures, there are signs that other states are moving cautiously to develop non-Russian options. In January 2007, Gazprom demanded huge price increases from Azerbaijan and Georgia. Azerbaijan, which used to import Russian gas despite its own vast resources, declined a Gazprom price increase and sped up the development of its own infrastructure. It also cut oil exports via the Russian-owned pipeline to Novorossiisk. Simultaneously, an agreement among Georgia, Azerbaijan and Turkey gave Georgia additional gas from the Shah Deniz field [in Azerbaijan] in order to make up for the shortfall. Other gas-rich states also seem ready to assist Georgia. At a March 2007 meeting between Georgian President Mikhail Saakashvili and his Kazakh counterpart, Nursultan Nazarbaev, it was announced that Kazakhstan was considering building a refinery in Georgia.

Kazakhstan has pursued a measured policy, careful not to alienate Russia. Its first major export pipeline was the Caspian Pipeline Consortium project, which carries Kazakh oil across Russia to Novorossiisk. Recently, in addition to the support for Georgia, Kazakhstan has announced plans to develop a new oil terminal in Kuryk. The $3 billion project, to be funded by Chevron, Exxon, LUKarco and others, will facilitate oil shipments across the Caspian. These future trans-Caspian shipments will fill the Baku-Tbilisi-Ceyhan pipeline—the first completed non-Russian export route. This fall, Kazakhstan and China signed an agreement extending an already existing pipeline to the Caspian in order to increase volumes of oil flowing to China. Finally, both Kazakhstan and Azerbaijan rejected a Russian proposal at the October Caspian summit that would have blocked trans-Caspian pipeline construction.

As for Europe, the crises with transit states Ukraine and Belarus alerted the European Union to the dangers of over-reliance on Russia for oil and gas supplies. For its part, Gazprom and Rosneft, the state-owned oil company, are hoping to reassure Europe by constructing new pipelines, most notably Nordstream, to bypass the recalcitrant ex-Soviet republics. But this reassurance is diminished by Gazprom's acquisition (or attempted acquisition) of European pipeline and refining assets. The picture is made even more complicated by the reality that no matter how much President Putin berates the Europeans,[17] Gazprom and Europe are co-dependent. Analysts estimate that more than 80 percent of Russia's oil exports and almost all of its gas exports go to Europe.[18] Thus, nearly all of the petro-dollar windfall of the past few years is derived from the European market. Moreover, Gazprom is Russia's largest earner of hard currency, and its tax revenues contribute one-quarter of Russia's tax coffers.

Prospectively, what is in question is Gazprom's use of those revenues. Gazprom's attempts to snap up assets in Europe indicate that it is not using its huge revenues to invest in green fields and to refurbish decaying pipelines. This leaves Gazprom dependent on cheap gas from Central Asia, especially from Turkmenistan. Second, even if Gazprom were to invest more wisely, would those revenues go to develop fields and infrastructure to supply the European market, or would they go to developing sources in eastern Siberia and infrastructure to feed the growing Asian markets? A wise investment strategy—

one that would increase export capacity and develop new fields in both eastern and western Siberia—requires a steady revenue stream. In effect this means that should Europe successfully find new suppliers, the money available to the Russian state to build new pipelines would be limited. Putin implicitly acknowledged this by repeatedly calling for security of demand, and as noted earlier, Aleksandr Medvedev has threatened huge price increases.

The bottom line is that Russia possesses huge amounts of oil and natural gas, but the legacies of poor investment decisions and neglect of infrastructure hamper its export capacity. Russia may want to use its energy clout, but its neighbors and customers further afield are increasingly wary of its political ambitions. Thus, Russia is indeed an energy colossus, but it is a giant with limited reach and standing on only one foot.

Footnotes

1. See discussion in Michael Fredholm, "Gazprom in Crisis: Putin's Quest for State Planning and Russia's Growing Natural Gas Deficit," Conflict Studies Research Center, Oct. 2006, http://www.defac.ac.uk/colleges/csrc. See also, "The Energy Strategy of Russia for the Period up to 2020," Decree # 1234R, Aug. 28, 2003.
2. See the discussion in Harley Balzer, "Vladimir Putin's Academic Writings and Russian National Resources Policy," Problems of Post-Communism, January/February (2006), pp. 48-54.
3. Stephen Boykewich, "The Man with the Plan for Russia Inc.," Moscow Times.com, June 6, 2006, accessed at http://www.themoscowtimes.com/stories/2006/06/06/002.html.
4. Andrew Monoghan, "Russia and the Security of Europe's Energy Supplies: Security in Diversity?" Conflict Studies Research Center, January 2007, http://www.defac.ac.uk/colleges/csrc.
5. Sarah Leitner, "EU's Tough Energy Plans Prompt Moscow Concerns," Financial Times, September 20, 2007, available at http://www.ft.com/cms/s/0/78dcf396 -6712-11dc-a218-0000779fd2ac.html.
6. Catherine Bolton, "Gazprom Chief Warns Brussels on Price Rise Risk," Financial Times, Nov. 21, 2007, p. 2.
7. Milov notes further that China will import between 20-25 billion cubic meters of natural gas, but liquefied natural gas from Sakhalin II, for example, has been fully contracted to Japan, the US, and Korea. Vladimir Milov, "Neo-Con Plans and the Sober Reality," Russia in Global Affairs, Vol. 4, No. 4 (2006), p. 125, 128.
8. Energy Information Agency, "Country Analysis Brief/Russia," updated April 2007, www.eia.doe.gov/ cabs/Russia.
9. Energy Information Agency, "Country Analysis Brief/Russia."

10. Fredholm, "Gazprom in Crisis . . ." p. 9.
11. Elena Shishkunova, "Herman Gref: Soon the Whole Economy will Start to Cough," Izvestiia, Nov. 2, 2006, p. 7, http://site.securities.com.ezp1.harvard.edu/doc.html?pc=RU&doc_id=118087458, and Fredholm, "Gazprom in Crisis . . ." p. 9.
12. See, for example, Oksana Gavshina, "Western Companies to be Permitted to Develop Shtokman," Gazeta, July 10, 2007, p. 12.
13. Energy Information Agency brief on the Caspian Region, available at www.eia.doe.gov, updated Jan. 2007.
14. The five Caspian littoral states have met repeatedly to settle bilateral disputes and to agree on a demarcation scheme for the inland sea. By all accounts the most recent meeting, at the heads of state level, was the most productive to date. Nonetheless, there is still no agreement on the sectoral division of the sea. At the meeting, Russia made a bid, rebuffed by Azerbaijan and Kazakhstan, to block trans-Caspian pipelines.
15. Discussions with western officials in Ashgabat, Turkmenistan, Oct. 2007.
16. Robin Pagnamenta, "UK Secures Energy Deal with Regime in Turkmenistan," Times, Nov. 6, 2007, accessed at timesonline.co.uk.
17. "Putin Snipes at EU on Access to Assets," Moscow Times, Oct. 29, 2007, p. 2, accessed at www.themoscowtimes.com.
18. Although somewhat outdated, the estimates contained in Fiona Hill's Brookings paper are illustrative. See Fiona Hill, "Beyond Co-Dependency: European Reliance on Russian Energy," The Brookings Institution, US-Europe Analysis Series, July 2005, available at www.brookings.edu.

*"An alliance with Russia is in our inter-
est."*

The United States
Should View Russia as
a Strategic Partner

Gary Hart

*In the following viewpoint, Gary Hart says a confrontational
stance toward Russia is a big mistake. His argument is based on
American self-interest: A positive relationship "is not a favor to
the Russians but an advantage to us." Hart cites five ways the
United States benefits from a partnership with Russia: Nuclear
arsenals can be reduced; the war on terrorism will be more effective; oil supplies will be more predictable; American technology
will have a potentially huge new market; and Russia would be
uniquely positioned to influence Middle Eastern politics in
America's favor. Besides, Hart says, our only hope of solving
twenty-first-century global problems, such as climate change and
pandemics, is with the cooperation of the world's major powers.
Gary Hart, now a professor at the University of Colorado Den-
ver School of Public Affairs, was a U.S. senator from Colorado
from 1975 to 1987 and a Democratic candidate for president in
1984 and 1988.*

As you read, consider the following questions:

1. What does Hart mean when he says that the current animosity between the United States and Russia is "a chicken-and-egg syndrome?"

2. How would a strategic partnership between Russia and the United States help defeat terrorism, in the author's view? How would it reduce the United States' dependence on Persian Gulf oil?

3. According to Hart, which three regional powers are critical to future world stability?

This letter is an appeal [for] a more positive, constructive relationship between the United States and Russia—less for Russia than for the United States.

At virtually any point between 1947 and 1991, if any serious thinker had proposed that we could form a strategic relationship with Russia but should refuse to do so, he or she would have been considered misguided at best and slightly deranged at worst. Yet that has happened today. The mystery is this: What forces are at work to demonize Russia, to isolate and alienate it from the West and to treat it as an enemy?

What Drives Russia and the U.S. Apart?

Few would dispute that Russia has become increasingly imperious and autocratic, though almost always in internal affairs and neighboring states. [Russian president from 2000 to 2008] Vladimir Putin has re-centralized power. Only history can determine, however, whether this is a reaction to Western, especially American, actions or whether it reflects the Russian character. But undoubtedly a chicken-egg syndrome exists: The more U.S. actions isolate the Russians, the more Moscow seeks to recapture its independent great-power status. . . .

[Two recent] developments on the U.S. side stand out. First is the policy of the [George W.] Bush Administration, largely promoted by Vice President Richard Cheney, to adopt a confrontational stance toward Russia. Cheney, among others has advocated using NATO as an anti-Russian military alliance.[1] He and others have also proposed overt support to Putin's domestic political opponents.

Second, more surprisingly, is an unreflective reaction among foreign policy elites, particularly the Council on Foreign Relations [CFR, a nonpartisan, nongovernmental advisory board], to endorse this policy. The CFR report's executive summary might as well have read: "The poor state of the U.S.-Russia relationship is entirely the fault of the Russians, who refuse to conduct their domestic affairs as we insist they should. We should hold the Russians to a uniquely high standard, though we refuse to say why."

Still, no argument is given to justify this animosity. Whatever the reason—lingering nostalgia for the Cold War's relative clarity, desire for a tangible nation-state opponent in a world of stateless terrorism—it should be set forth. The best the CFR can do is decry the various failures of the Russians to meet liberal democratic standards. Those standards apply uniquely to the Russians.

Numerous Russia experts, including Stephen Cohen at New York University, Anatol Lieven at the New America Foundation and Graham Allison at Harvard's Kennedy School, have challenged what they perceive as a concerted effort to alienate Russia from the West. It would astonish any objective observer that the Jackson-Vanik Amendment, a 1974 measure denying most favored nation trading status (now called normal trade relations) to Russia as leverage to liberate dissidents and refuseniks [those refused permission to emigrate during the Soviet era], is still official U.S. policy. Its repeal would represent an excellent beginning point in putting U.S.-Russian relations on a more productive track.

1. NATO stands for the North Atlantic Treaty Organization, a military alliance of twenty-six countries. Russia is a partner in the NATO-Russia Council created in 2002 but is *not* a NATO member.

The U.S.-Russia Strategic Framework Declaration

The era in which the United States and Russia considered one another an enemy or strategic threat has ended. We reject the zero-sum thinking of the Cold War when "what was good for Russia was bad for America" and vice versa. Rather, we are dedicated to working together and with other nations to address the global challenges of the 21st century, moving the U.S.-Russia relationship from one of strategic competition to strategic partnership. We intend to cooperate as partners to promote security, and to jointly counter the threats to peace we face, including international terrorism and the proliferation of weapons of mass destruction. We are determined to build a lasting peace, both on a bilateral basis and in international fora, recognizing our shared responsibility to the people of our countries and the global community of nations to remain steadfast and united in pursuit of international security, and a peaceful, free world. Where we have differences, we will work to resolve them in a spirit of mutual respect. . . .

We will work together to address serious differences in areas where our policies do not coincide, including NATO expansion; development of a package solution that helps restore the viability of the CFE [Conventional Armed Forces in Europe] regime and prompt ratification of the Adapted CFE Treaty by all the States' Parties; and certain military activities in space.

The White House, Office of the Press Secretary,
"U.S.-Russia Strategic Framework Declaration,"
April 6, 2008.

What Are Russia's and America's Common Interests?

"What interests, if any, do we have in common?" should be our first question. There are several. First, we have an ongoing interest in reducing nuclear arsenals. Thanks to the persistent efforts of former Senator Sam Nunn (D-GA) and Senator Richard Lugar (R-IN), and despite resistance by the [George W.] Bush Administration, we continue working to dramatically reduce both sides' nuclear warhead and delivery system stockpiles. A serious argument against this project has yet to surface.

Second, we have a mutual interest in defeating terrorism. The Russians have conducted prolonged military actions in Chechnya, and the United States has conducted equally prolonged military occupations of Afghanistan and Iraq. There are clear differences in methodology, with the Russians using much more brutal means, but the residents of Grozny [the now-devastated capital of Chechnya] and of Fallujah might not see that. Though opposing our invasion of Iraq, the Russians fully endorsed our invasion of Afghanistan (where they themselves had a rather unpleasant experience). If we are not fully exploiting Russian intelligence networks in pursuit of this common interest, it is to our detriment.

Third, there is the matter of oil. During the first [Bill] Clinton Administration, I urged our government to negotiate long-term oil purchase agreements with the Russians to help reduce our dependence on dangerously unstable Persian Gulf sources. It is not too late for that. The Russians need massive Western investment in oil production facilities, and the United States and its European allies need predictable oil supplies. High-level diplomatic and commercial engagement with the Russians can prevent destructive Russian tendencies to nationalize oil production facilities. There is no reason we cannot replicate our decades-long arrangements, such as those with the Saudis, in Russia, but this will require stable, friendly relations.

Fourth, we have high technology, and the Russians need it, particularly in telecommunications, health care and industrial modernization. A decade of experience modernizing Russia's telecommunication system convinces me of two things: 21st-century communications technology is key to Russia's emerging economy, and Russian science, though inadequately equipped, has much to offer the West and global markets. Russia represents a huge potential market for U.S. technology companies—its health care system is abysmal for most Russians—and U.S. companies should be encouraged to explore those markets.

Fifth, Russia is neighbor to several Islamic states, former Soviet republics—whether one subscribes to a Huntingtonian thesis of civilization clashes [political scientist Samuel Huntington's theory that religious and cultural issues will be the major conflicts in the post–Cold War world] or merely believes in civilization frictions, Russia occupies an unrivaled strategic position. Further, it occupies a strategic position in northeast Asia, particularly with regard to North Korea and China. As the noted Russia expert Dimitri Simes has repeatedly pointed out, Russia's geostrategic location places it in a unique position to exert influence on critical matters such as Iran's nuclear ambitions. An alliance with Russia is in our interest.

How the U.S. Benefits

This list of shared interests is far from exhaustive, and several principles should guide a constructive bilateral relationship. Mutual self-interest, not altruism, is one. A working relationship is not a favor to the Russians but an advantage to us. Russia is by history and culture a Western nation and should be integrated into the West. The United States and Russia share security interests and concerns. An isolated, anti-democratic Russia increases our insecurity. Russia's development as a market democracy will best be achieved by engagement, not rejection.

Until recent years, when U.S. foreign policy assumed a theological aura, we consistently sought self-interested relations with disagreeable nations. The late [ambassador to the United Nations under Ronald Reagan] Jeane Kirkpatrick is notable for distinguishing authoritarian states, with whom we could collaborate, from totalitarian states with which we could have nothing to do. Even today, despite strong emphasis on good and evil, we maintain productive relations with states no less authoritarian than Russia (including former Soviet republics).

Also, to expect Russian subservience to its chief Cold War rival is to misunderstand Russian history, culture and character. At few points in U.S. history, prior to the end of the Cold War, have we adopted the imperious attitude toward other nations that we have in the 21st century. Not coincidentally, this arrogance arrived with a neo-imperialist project that has overtaken our foreign policy.

Few nations rival Russia in nationalist sentiment. Though younger Russians with income are internationalist and cosmopolitan, outside Moscow and among older generations "Mother Russia" is still a palpable phenomenon. Dictation of domestic behavior and performance, especially by the United States, is a sure prescription for popular resistance. In most cases, the issue is not what is preferable, best and right, but who is dictating it. U.S. policymakers, including Democratic congressional majorities, must not treat the Russians as schoolchildren.

Twenty-first-century realities require we get all the help we can. These realities include WMD [weapons of mass destruction] proliferation, terrorism, failed and failing states, tribalism, ethnic nationalism, religious fundamentalism, the decline of nation-state sovereignty, integrating markets, climate change and the threat of pandemics. One nation alone cannot solve these problems. It is not in America's national interest, and particularly its security interests, to go it alone or rely on "coalitions of the willing" composed of minor powers rallied *in extremis*.

How the World Benefits

On the U.S. Commission on National Security for the 21st Century [Hart is a former co-chair], my fellow commissioners and I agreed unanimously that three regional powers are critical to future world stability. These were China, India and Russia. We urged the new Bush Administration in early 2001, and thereafter, to expand ties to these nations, contribute more to regional stability and encourage economic and political leadership. No systematic effort has been made to implement these recommendations; in the case of Russia the opposite has occurred.

In a [January 2008] *Wall Street Journal* opinion piece, "A Nuclear-Free World," former Secretary of State George Shultz, former Secretary of Defense William Perry, former Secretary of State Henry Kissinger and former Senator Sam Nunn set forth an ambitious agenda to eliminate nuclear weapons. This is impossible absent Russian cooperation, which will be easier to engage if relations are positive and productive.

Congress does not make foreign policy. The congressional party, particularly in opposition, is hamstrung if the executive branch shuts it out from offering advice and consent. But Congress can educate the American people on the importance of a constructive relationship with Russia. That is what I advocate here.

Administration officials should develop a positive U.S.-Russian relationship or, if they refuse, defend that position. In recent years this has not happened. The 110th Congress should undertake this project. The United States does not have the luxury of creating unnecessary conflicts. We have enough to deal with as it is. It is not in our interest to demonize and isolate Russia; it *is* in our interest to integrate it into the West.

> "U.S.-Russian relations are clearly far
> from . . . [an] authentic partnership.
> For the foreseeable future it will be all
> but impossible to put relations on such
> a footing."

The United States Should Not View Russia as a Strategic Partner

John Edwards and Jack Kemp

In the following viewpoint, John Edwards and Jack Kemp argue that there is so much rivalry and disagreement between the United States and Russia that a strategic partnership is highly unlikely. They portray Russia as antidemocratic, anti-Western, uncooperative on energy issues, and willing to deal militarily with China at America's expense. This viewpoint is excerpted from a 2006 report by the Council on Foreign Relations' task force on U.S.-Russia relations chaired by the authors. The Council on Foreign Relations is a nonpartisan foreign policy think tank based in New York and Washington, D.C. Jack Kemp is a political consultant and former Republican U.S. representative

Russia's Wrong Direction: What the United States Can and Should Do, Independent Task Force Report No. 57, New York, NY: Council on Foreign Relations, 2006. Copyright © 2006 by the Council on Foreign Relations, Inc. All rights reserved. Reproduced by permission.

and John Edwards was a Democratic U.S. senator and presidential candidate in 2004 and 2008.

As you read, consider the following questions:

1. What three key conditions of a strategic partnership do Russia and the United States lack, according to the authors?

2. Edwards and Kemp argue that the United States should try harder to work with Russia only when the cost of *not* working with Russia is extremely high. In their view, what two vital national-security issues are worth cooperating on?

3. What do Edwards and Kemp consider the most important obstacle to future cooperation between Russia and the United States?

Russian and American leaders have for many years used the hopeful term "partnership"—and often the still grander one, "strategic partnership"—to describe their vision for relations between Moscow and Washington. Reality has, with brief exceptions, usually been more modest. Russia and the United States have only very rarely acted as partners in any meaningful sense of the word. When they have cooperated, it has been because their interests on this or that narrow issue were sufficiently similar to allow them to work together. But cumulative effects—an accretion of trust, the habit of joint action, a spillover to other issues—have been few.

Why There Is No Genuine Partnership Now

What would a genuine U.S.-Russian partnership require? It would go beyond similar assessments of specific international problems and opportunities.

- It would rest on a conviction that, while great nations have their differences on specific issues, their strategic interests are so similar that neither has to fear—or seek to undermine—the other.

- It would be strengthened by mutual confidence that the other side is willing to commit resources to deal with new challenges, that its institutions can be counted on to perform effectively, and that disagreements will be addressed through candid discussion and are not the expression of unspoken goals and resentments.

- Strong common interest would lie at the heart of such a relationship, but only a strong common outlook would make it succeed.

Looked at in this light, U.S.-Russian relations are clearly far from meeting the conditions of authentic partnership. For the foreseeable future it will be all but impossible to put relations on such a footing. The mutual confidence that partnership requires is missing. When Russia and the United States work together it is likely to be a matter of case-by-case, carefully circumscribed cooperation....

Why Relations Are Likely to Get Worse

On the high-priority issue of Iran, cooperation may continue; on other issues, increased disagreement and rivalry are likely.

The list of factors that can negatively shape the relationship is too long to justify any other forecast:

- The Russian electoral calendar means that the political tightening of the recent past has probably not run its full course. [Vladimir] Putin [then president] and his advisers are leaving much less to chance than [former President] Boris Yeltsin did as he approached the end of his second term in 1999, and their approach will keep dramatizing Russia's status outside the mainstream of modern democratic politics.

- Russia's policies toward virtually all its neighbors are increasingly animated by a spirit of competition with the West in general and with the United States in particular, and by a greater willingness to jeopardize cooperation with both the United States and major European states. Though several episodes have now cast Moscow in the worst possible light, this approach continues. It seems to guide Russian policy toward the so-called "frozen conflicts"—unresolved separatist conflicts in other post-Soviet states. In several of these, Russia is the principal source of external support for separatist forces. . . .

- Russian energy policy has turned a prized asset of economic relations into a potential tool of political intimidation. Russian officials make no secret of their belief that their country's commanding position in world energy markets should help advance its political objectives. The [2006] cutoff of gas supplies to Ukraine has been the most shocking and coercive application of this view to date, but others may lie ahead.

- Increasing sales of arms and advanced military technologies to China—and Russo-Chinese efforts to make small gains at American expense—mean a growing divergence between Russian policy, on the one hand, and U.S. and European policy, on the other. . . .

- Russia faces what one of [former] President Putin's senior political advisers calls an "underground fire" in the North Caucasus—made worse by the unending war with [part of its own federation, the republic of] Chechnya—and its vulnerability to major terrorist incidents in that region and across Russia remains high. A problem that ought to encourage U.S.-Russian cooperation is made divisive by Moscow's preference for blaming outsiders—even the West—and by its embrace of repressive strategies elsewhere in the former Soviet Union.

Russia Still Has Imperialist Ambitions

For most of the past 15 years, the response to Russian actions by the United States and Europe has been driven by their perceptions of Russian reform. Western policy seems to be based on the premise that peaceful evolution can be ensured by democracy and by concentrating Russia's energies on developing a market economy. Western diplomacy has thus seen its main task as strengthening Russian reform. . . .

But a far more important factor than reform is Russia's attempt to restore its preeminence in the territories it once controlled. The Russia that emerged from the collapse of the Soviet Union on Christmas Day 1991 came with borders that reflect no historical precedent. Accordingly, Russia is devoting much of its energy to restoring political influence in, if not control of, its lost empire.

Yuliya Tymoshenko, former prime minister of Ukraine, "Containing Russia," Foreign Affairs, *May–June 2007.*

Three Kinds of Problems to Solve

A relationship that has to deal with a list of problems like this one is more likely to get worse than it is to get better. If so, American policy will face the challenge of trying to deal with three very different kinds of problems.

- First, the United States needs to do more to promote cooperation with Russia on those issues where the cost of not working together is especially high and a constructive result remains a realistic possibility.

- Second, where Russian policy is becoming less positive, the United States needs a response that recognizes the change and adjusts to it. American policy has to explore expanded cooperation on issues where Russia is prepared to make itself part of the solution, but it cannot count on hopes for cooperation in those cases where Russia has become part of the problem.

- Finally, there are issues where the gap between the U.S. approach and that of Russia has become so wide that cooperation is unlikely and where good results can be achieved only by drawing a clearer line between U.S. interests and values and those reflected in current Russian policy.

American policy toward Russia has to become more selective, and the approach the United States selects will vary from issue to issue. Iran and nuclear security are prime examples of problems in the first of the three categories above—issues of vital national-security importance where effective U.S.-Russian cooperation can be facilitated by an expanded effort.

- On issues like Iran and the security of dangerous nuclear materials, Russia has shown strong, sometimes even resentful sensitivity to American efforts to shape its policies and practices, but it has also revealed an underlying common interest that makes joint action possible.

- In both of these cases, there is little—or, in the case of nuclear security, no—chance of getting a satisfactory result without Russian participation.

The United States needs a different approach for dealing with problems in the second category, in which potential common interests may be giving way to greater discord. Energy security is one such issue.

- Energy cooperation with Russia was once seen as a new and direct route to increased global energy security, but it has now become an area of tension as well. An effective policy needs to reflect both these realities.

- True energy security can be advanced by increased Western participation in the development of Russia's vast resources. At the same time, it is inconsistent with a system of corporate governance that makes Russia's strategic resources a day-to-day political tool to be used by Kremlin officials. This system makes politically motivated energy cut-offs a permanent possibility and makes it impossible to treat Russia's state-owned companies as though they were commercial entities. . . .

Finally, there are those problems on which American policy needs to recognize how sharp the differences between U.S. interests and policies and Russia's have, unfortunately, become. Here we refer to two issues—Russia's relations with its neighbors and the growing authoritarianism of its political institutions. Neither of these is a new issue in U.S.-Russian relations, but in the past the two sides have generally been able to avoid dealing with them directly and divisively. Now latent disagreement has become more open and destructive, and the two issues have become intertwined. . . .

The Main Obstacle

In the next several years the most important negative factor in U.S.-Russian relations is likely to be Russia's emergent authoritarian political system. This trend will make it harder for the two sides to find common ground and harder to cooperate even when they do. It makes the future direction of Russian politics much less predictable.

If Russia remains on an authoritarian course, U.S.-Russian relations will almost certainly continue to fall short of their potential. Even today Russia's economic revival, political stability, and international self-confidence ought to have led to expanded cooperation on many fronts. Yet what has emerged instead is a relationship with a very narrow base. The large common interests that might animate a real partnership, including energy, counterterrorism, and nonproliferation, are frequently subordinated to other concerns of Russian policy—to internal struggles over property and power, to sensitivity about Russia's influence on its periphery, to anxieties about its looming political transition.

> *"Moscow . . . is once again asserting it-self in the [Middle East], seeking to re-vive its superpower status of the Soviet era."*

Russia's Influence in the Middle East Is Growing

Ed Blanche

In the following viewpoint, Ed Blanche argues that Moscow is using Muslim hostility toward the United States, which has grown sharply since the invasion of Iraq in 2003, as an opportunity to reassert Russian influence in the region. The biggest prize, according to Blanche, is key U.S. ally Saudi Arabia, but Russia is also trying to establish closer links with Saudi rival Iran and aligning itself with the Palestinian Hamas. Blanche sees this as a zero-sum game—U.S. influence weakens as Russian influence grows. Note that this piece was written while Vladimir Putin was still president of Russia, and it remains to be seen if the course he was steering will change with new president Dmitry Medvedev, who took office in May of 2008. Ed Blanche is a Beirut-based journalist who has covered Middle East affairs for three decades and is a member of the International Institute for Strategic Studies in London.

Ed Blanche, "Claws of the Bear," *The Middle East,* April 2007, pp. 6, 9–10. Copyright © 2007 IC Publications. Reproduced by permission.

As you read, consider the following questions:

1. Commentators disagree about the intent of Vladimir Putin's 2007 speech outlining Russia's strategy in the Middle East. What did Putin say?

2. How is Russia exerting its influence in Iran, according to Blanche?

3. What is Russia's main tool in building ties with Saudi Arabia, Syria, Egypt, Iraq, Libya, and Yemen, according to the author?

During the decades of confrontation between East and West, the Americans and Russians used the constant wars in the Middle East as a laboratory for their weapons systems and military doctrines: the Israelis fighting with US arms, the Arabs with Soviet hardware.

What the Israelis call their Second Lebanon War, fought during the dog days of July and August 2006, turned out to be more of the same, although the Russians were not directly arming Hizbullah [or Hezbollah, a Lebanon anti-Israel militia and political party] themselves. Iran and Syria, two states reliant on Russian arms, provided the missiles and rockets that allowed Hizbullah to fight the Israelis to a standstill.

A New Cold War?

But that 34-day conflict underlined how Moscow, its coffers brimming with enormous oil and gas revenues, is once again asserting itself in the region, seeking to revive its superpower status of the Soviet era to counter the US in what some see as a new Cold War.

[Russian president Vladimir] Putin threw down the gauntlet to the US with his forceful speech at the 43rd Munich Security Conference in February [2007]. "Unipolarity is not only unacceptable but is also impossible in today's world," he declared, defining that as a situation in which there is "one centre of force, one centre of decision-making . . . one master, one sovereign."

He went on: "I am convinced that we have reached the decisive moment when we must seriously think about the architecture of global security. We must proceed by searching for a reasonable balance between the interests of all participants in the international dialogue."

The Americans were flabbergasted. Some US commentators saw Putin's speech as the declaration of a new Cold War. But veteran Middle East analyst Patrick Seale disagrees: "This is a mistake."

He wrote in the pan-Arab *Al Hayat* newspaper, "It is a call for a healthier multi-polar international system, based on a balance of power and underpinned by a balance of deterrence, in which conflicts are resolved not exacerbated, in which the strong are contained and the weak no longer live in fear."

Many disagree with Moscow's new strategy. Yulia Tymoshenko, former prime minister of Ukraine and currently leader of its opposition, argues that "Russian policy, based on immediate monetary gain and hope of diplomatic influence, is dangerously short-sighted. . . .

"By enfeebling diplomacy, Russia is taking the world into more dangerous territory. . . . This is doubly short-sighted as a nuclear-armed Iran on Russia's border is not in Russia's national interest, particularly with Russia's own 20 [million] Muslim citizens becoming increasingly radicalised."

Whether a new Cold War is indeed in the making remains to be seen, but Putin's speech certainly evoked echoes of that costly 50-year ideological struggle and definitively marked the demise of the often uneasy post-9/11 alliance between Moscow and Washington. Putin's analysis, according to *Jane's Intelligence Digest*, "amounted to little more than a diatribe against US foreign policy, particularly in the Middle East."

Arab Countries Are Rooting for the Rise of Russia

The Arab and Iranian press have been rooting for the return and rise of Russia in the Middle East. . . .

An editorial titled "Moscow Maneuvering to Regain Former Status" in the December 21 [2006] issue of the *Tehran Times* discussed the hopes of Russia restoring "the international status Moscow enjoyed during the Cold War" and added, "Amid tensions in the Middle East, Russia is trying to regain its former role in the region. . . . The main goal of these activities is restoring Russia's international status, which was greatly diminished after the collapse of the Soviet Union. . . . If Moscow can pull that off, Russia can establish a balance of power in the strategic Middle East region to counter U.S. influence."

Steven Stalinsky,
"The Middle East Cheers the Rise of Russia,"
New York Sun, *January 12, 2007.*

Anti-Americanism Helps Russia

Following the collapse of the Soviet Union, the region fell firmly within the US orbit. But since 9/11, and particularly since the ill-starred March 2003 invasion of Iraq, Muslim hostility has mushroomed and Moscow, having regained much of the confidence lost with the Soviet collapse nearly two decades ago, has seen this as an opening to be exploited to the hilt.

Russia's new assertive foreign policy rests in large part on the extent to which Putin, a former colonel in the KGB [the Soviet Union's Security agency, secret police and intelligence agency from 1954 to 1991] has packed the senior echelons of the Russian leadership with veterans or serving members of the Soviet intelligence community. A study of the leadership conducted under the auspices of Russia's respected Academy of Sciences, released in December 2006, showed that 80% of the top posts were held by such people.

Prominent among them is Putin's close political ally Sergei Ivanov, the former defence minister promoted to first deputy prime minister. . . . Ivanov, a diehard reserve colonel-general in the FSB, the KGB's successor agency, who in 2003 declared that Russia did not rule out a pre-emptive strike anywhere in the world if the national interest demanded it, is the frontrunner to succeed Putin as president when his term expires in March 2008. [Instead, Putin was succeeded by Dmitry Medvedev.] That would assure the continuance of Moscow's aggressive new foreign policy strategy.

Another former KGB officer with a key post in Putin's leadership cadre is Sergei Chemezov, who heads the state-owned arms company Rosoboronexport, which has defied the US and Israel by selling advanced missiles of various kinds to Iran and Syria—some of which have ended up in Hizbullah's armoury.

Trying to Build Relations with Both Iran and Saudi Arabia

Saudi Arabia is the big prize for Russia. Putin's groundbreaking visit to the kingdom—and to Qatar and Jordan—immediately after the Munich conference underlined his efforts to forge a new relationship with a key longtime US ally in the Middle East, probably the most significant of all Moscow's strategic targets in the region. Russia has already invested much time and effort in establishing close links with Iran, whose influence has been strengthened because of Moscow's support.

Iran and Saudi Arabia are vying for leadership of the Muslim world, and Russia's strategy will entail some deft footwork if it is to maintain strong relations with both Riyadh [Saudi Arabia] and Tehran [Iran]. According to the Texas-based think-tank Strategic Forecasting, "The Kremlin knows it must position itself among the Arabs to really use the Middle East as a lever in its struggle with the US.

"The Russians are aware that the Saudis think the US position in the region is weakening, and that Riyadh has grown wary of US policies there, which have empowered rival Iran. In fact, Putin's visit to Saudi Arabia is in part the result of Riyadh's assistance to Moscow to help quell the jihadist insurgency in [Russia's own troubled province] Chechnya."

The Saudis seek to widen their foreign policy options because as American power evaporates in the region they need to make other arrangements for their security. There are serious differences between Moscow and Riyadh over oil production, but the Saudis hope that by establishing closer links with Russia, the kingdom will be better able to counter Iran and Syria, both aided by Moscow.

Until recently, the Russians had focused primarily on building up relations with internationally-isolated Iran and incurred US wrath by providing crucial aid for its nuclear energy programme, which Washington says cloaks a clandestine drive to develop nuclear weapons.

The Russians are completing Iran's first nuclear reactor at Bushehr on the northern [Persian] Gulf coast under an $800 [million] contract and have said they are ready to build four more. Iran is also a key arms customer and this has given Moscow considerable weight in Tehran, which it says it has used to encourage Iran to moderate its position in negotiations with the United Nations on this dangerous issue. Time will tell on that.

Russia's Role in an Arab-Israeli Peace Settlement

Russia also holds an important diplomatic card in the Middle East as a member of the so-called Quartet—the others are the US, the European Union and the UN—that seeks to promote an Arab-Israeli peace settlement.

But Moscow's current strategy of supporting the Palestinian Islamic Resistance Movement Hamas in its political role as part of the Palestine National Authority with the rival Fatah movement, is causing a widening gulf within the Quartet and could stymie efforts to stitch together a unity government. (Originally a resistance movement, the political arm of Hamas won a majority of seats in the Palestinian parliament in 2006.)

The February [2007] talks held in Moscow with Hamas's leader, Khaled Meshaal, indicate the Kremlin is determined to pursue its own agenda as regards the peace process.

This may involve moving away from brokering a peace deal as part of the Quartet. That would be consistent with Putin's ambition of rebuilding Russian influence in the region at the expense of the US and the EU [European Union].

Arms Sales

One of the Russians' main tools in their push into the Middle East is the export of arms—much as it was during the Soviet era. Moscow has said it is prepared to assist Riyadh in developing nuclear power—just as it has with Iran—but that is not likely to happen for some time, if indeed at all. Moscow has extended the same offer to Egypt and Algeria, raising US hackles over fears that nuclear energy projects could lead to nuclear arms programmes, as the US says is happening in Iran.

In late August 2006, a team of Russian military experts visited Saudi Arabia to discuss the possible sale of T-95 main battle tanks and Mi-17 helicopters. That was a significant breakthrough for the Russians. The Saudis have traditionally bought their weapons systems from the US, as well as to a lesser extent from Britain and France.

Although there is no expectation that Riyadh will start buying Russian arms any time soon, it has been seeking to diversify its arms suppliers of late to reduce dependence on the US. Riyadh bought Chinese CSS-1 East Wind nuclear-capable ballistic missiles in 1988.

With the Americans tied down in Iraq and Afghanistan, Moscow sees an opportunity to revive its Cold War arms deals with its old clients in the Middle East, Syria, Egypt, Iraq, Libya and Yemen. Major deals have been struck, with Moscow sweetening the pot by writing off much of the huge military debts these countries ran up during the Cold War. Algeria, for instance, recently signed a $7 [billion] deal for fighter aircraft, tanks and air-defence missiles.

The sale to Iran and Syria of advanced surface-to-air and anti-tank missile systems, along with other equipment such as thermal imaging systems for night-fighting, has incensed the US and Israel.

Sophisticated anti-armour missiles such as the AT-14 Kornet-E and AT-13 Metis-M sold to Syria in recent years found their way to Hizbullah, which used them to devastating effect in the 2006 summer war. Israel has been particularly critical of Moscow's agreement to sell Syria AT-15 missiles that can penetrate the Jewish state's vaunted Merkava tanks.

Reports in 2005 that arms exporters Rosoboronexport planned to sell Pantsir S-1 and S-300 air-defence missile systems to Iran and Syria, as well as Su-30 strike aircraft to Syria via the former Soviet republic of Belarus, caused an international uproar. Such systems would seriously erode Israel's military superiority.

But Moscow went ahead with the $700 [million] sale of 29 Tor-M1 surface-to-air missiles to Iran, presumably to help protect its nuclear facilities from possible US or Israeli attack. Moscow had frequently used Belarus as a conduit for weapons sales to radical regimes.

> "Russia is doomed to a painful slide into geopolitical obsolescence and ultimately, perhaps even nonexistence."

Russia's Global Influence Is Shrinking

Peter Zeihan

In the following viewpoint, Peter Zeihan concludes that Russia is in political and economic decline. He blames the slide on two main factors. First, Ukraine, which Russia depends on for food imports, deep-water ports, and vital oil and gas transport routes, has broken away from Russian control and established constitutional, pro-Western reforms. Second, former president Vladimir Putin, whose hand-picked successor Dmitry Medvedev took office in May of 2008, spent so much effort wresting internal political and economic control from corrupt businessmen known as "oligarchs" that he turned Russia into an authoritarian state and neglected Russia's international interests. So the Kremlin is back in control internally, Zeihan says, but at great cost: Rich Western countries are less likely to invest in Russia's undemocratic society and more likely to encroach on Russian interests abroad. Peter Zeihan is a senior analyst with Strategic Forecasting (Stratfor), a private political, economic, and security consulting firm in Austin, Texas, that provides intelligence services to individuals, corporations, and U.S. and foreign governments.

As you read, consider the following questions:

1. According to Zeihan, what did Putin hope to achieve by putting so much effort into consolidating political and economic control?
2. What regions will be next to fall away from Russian influence, after Ukraine, in the author's view?
3. What does Zeihan mean when he describes Russia as "an earthquake society?"

Russia is in decline—politically, strategically, economically and demographically. The Commonwealth of Independent States [CIS, an alliance of eleven former Soviet republics], the only international organization that Moscow can rely upon to support it (and, incidentally, the one it dominates) is moribund because of lack of interest. The Americans are in Central Asia, and the other former Soviet republics are squirming out from under Moscow's grasp. Talk of a Russian-led Eurasian Economic Community that would reform the Soviet economy remains largely talk. Everything from Russia's early warning satellite system to its rank-and-file army is collapsing, with 90,000 troops unable to pacify [Russian republic] Chechnya even after five years of direct occupation. HIV and tuberculosis are spreading like wildfire, and the death rate stubbornly remains nearly double the birth rate, hampering Russia's ability even to field a nominal army or maintain a conventional work force.

Putin Versus the Oligarchs

[Former Russian president Vladimir] Putin realized that before he could reverse the decline, he had to consolidate control. One of [former president] Boris Yeltsin's greatest mistakes was that he lacked the authority to implement change. More to the point, no one feared Yeltsin, so the men who eventually became oligarchs [businessmen who became rich through connections with Russian government officials in the 1990s, when Russia switched to a market-based economy, away from communism] robbed the state blind, becoming power centers in and of themselves.

Putin spent the bulk of his first term reasserting control. The once-unruly (and a heavily oligarch-dominated) press has been subjugated to the state's will. Regional governors are now appointed directly by the president. Nearly all tax revenues flow into federal—not regional—coffers. The oligarchs ... are falling over each other to pay homage to Putin (at least publicly).

Putin systematically has worked to consolidate political control in the Kremlin as an institution and himself as a personality, using every development along the way to formalize his control over all levels of government and society. The result is a security state in which few dare oppose the will of the president-turned-czar.

From here, Putin hoped to revamp Russia's economic, legal and governmental structures sufficiently so that rule of law could take root, investors would feel safe and the West would—for its own reasons—fund the modernization of the Russian economy and state. Put another way, Putin was counting on his pro-Western orientation to be the deciding factor in ushering in a flood of Western investment to realize Russia's material riches and economic potential.

Putin's problem is that revamping the country's political and economic discourse required a massive amount of effort. The oligarchs, certainly not at first, did not wish to go quietly into that good night. ... During this time the Kremlin turned introspective, understandably obsessed with its effort to hammer domestic affairs into a more manageable form. Moreover, as Putin made progress and fewer oligarchs and bureaucrats were willing to challenge him, they also became too intimidated to act autonomously. The result was an ever-shrinking pool of people willing to speak up for fear of triggering Putin's wrath. The shrinking allotment of bandwidth forced Russia largely to ignore international developments, nearly collapsing its ability to monitor and protect its interests abroad.

This did not pass unnoticed.

Moscow's Foreign Policy Losses

Chinese penetration into the Russian Far East, European involvement in the economies of Russia's near abroad and U.S. military cooperation with former Soviet clients are at all-time highs. As Putin struggled to tame the Russian bear, Moscow racked up foreign policy losses in Central Asia, the Baltics, the Balkans and the Caucasus. Uzbekistan, Tajikistan and Kyrgyzstan all became U.S. allies. Serbia formally left Russia's sphere of influence, [former Soviet republic] Georgia welcomed U.S. troops with open arms and ejected a Russian-backed strongman from one of its separatist republics, and the three Baltic states and the bulk of the Warsaw Pact [Soviet-era alliance of communist states] joined both NATO and the European Union. And [in 2004] Ukraine [took] its first real steps away from Russia [when democratic opposition party Our Ukraine won the presidential election and sparked the peaceful "Orange Revolution" reforms, free of Russian control].

In short, Putin achieved the necessary focus to consolidate control, but the cost was the loss of not just the empire, but with Ukraine, the chance of one day rebuilding it.

More defeats are imminent. Once Ukraine adopts a less friendly relationship with Russia, the Russian deployment to Transdniestria—a tiny separatist republic in Moldova kept alive only by Russian largesse—will fade away. Next on the list will be the remaining Russian forces at Georgian bases at Akhalkalaki and Batumi. Georgia already has enacted an informal boycott on visa paperwork for incoming soldiers, and the United States has begun linking the Russian presence in Georgia and Transdniestria to broader Russian security concerns.

Once these outposts fall, Russia's only true international "allies" will be the relatively nonstrategic Belarus and Armenia, which the European Union and United States can be counted upon to hammer relentlessly.

To say Russia is at a turning point is a gross understatement. Without Ukraine, Russia is doomed to a painful slide into geopolitical obsolescence and ultimately, perhaps even nonexistence.

Russia has three roads before it.

Option 1: Accept the Whittling Away of Russia's Empire

Russia accepts the loss of Ukraine, soldiers on and hopes for the best. Should Putin accept the loss of Ukraine quietly and do nothing, he invites more encroachments—primarily Western—into Russia's dwindling sphere of influence and ultimately into Russia itself, assigning the country to a painful slide into strategic obsolescence. Never forget that Russia is a state formed by an expansionary military policy. The Karelian Isthmus of Russia's northwest once was Finnish territory, while the southern tier of the Russian Far East was once Chinese. Deep within the Russian "motherland" are the homelands of vibrant minorities such as the Tatars and the Bashkirs, who theoretically could survive on their own. Of course the North Caucasus is a region ripe for shattering; Chechens are not the only Muslims in the region with separatist desires.

Geopolitically, playing dead is an unviable proposition; domestically it could spell the end of the president. Putin rode to power on the nationalism of the Chechen war. His efforts to implement a Reaganesque ideal of Russian pride created a political movement that he has managed to harness, but never quite control. If Russian nationalists feel that his Westerniza-

Russia's Abandoned Positions

Guided by a realistic sense of self-limitation, the Putin administration has been reducing those vestiges of the Soviet world role which can no longer be sustained. [In 2003] its peacekeepers quietly left the Balkans; Moscow had to be content with a second-tier role in both the Korean and Iranian nuclear negotiations: its position in the Middle East quartet of countries dealing with the Israeli-Palestinian dispute has become largely nominal. Less voluntarily, Russia had to abandon its positions in Belgrade [Serbia] and Baghdad, which it had been using for a mediating role in relation to Washington. Russia's immediate foreign policy interest has shrunk to the former Soviet states.

Dmitri Trenin, "What You See Is What You Get,"
Carnegie Moscow Center, *May 4, 2004.*

tion efforts have signed bit after bit of the empire away with nothing in return, he could be overwhelmed by the creature he created. But Putin is a creature of logic and planning.

Though it might be highly questionable whether Putin could survive as Russia's leader if this path is chosen, the president's ironclad control of the state and society at this point would make his removal in favor of another path a complicated and perhaps protracted affair. With its economy, infrastructure, military and influence waning by the day, time is one thing Russia has precious little of.

Option 2: Push Back Against the West

Russia reassesses its geopolitical levers and pushes back against the West. Russia might have fallen a long way from its Soviet highs, but it still has a large number of hefty tools it can use to influence global events.

If Putin is to make the West rethink its strategy of rolling back Russian influence and options—not to mention safeguard his own skin—he will have to act in a way to remind the West that Moscow still has fight left in it and is far from out of options. And he will have to do it forcefully, obviously and quickly.

The dependence upon Ukraine goes both ways. While Ukraine's south and east are not majority Russian, those regions are heavily Russofied. Should a [reform-minded] Ukraine prove too hostile to Moscow, splitting a region that is linguistically, culturally and economically integrated into Russia off from Ukraine would not prove beyond Russia's means.

Also on the Ukrainian front, Russia has the energy card to play. [Ukrainian capital] Kiev's primary source of income is transit fees on natural gas and oil. Russia supplies about one-quarter of all European consumption. Tinkering with those supplies—or simply their delivery schedules—would throw the European economies into frenzy.

Russia could use its influence with Afghanistan's [anti-Taliban] Northern Alliance to make the United States' Afghan experience positively Russian. Sales of long-range cruise missiles in India or Sovremenny destroyers complete with Sunburn missiles to China would threaten U.S. control of the oceans. Weapons sales to Latin America would undermine U.S. influence in its own backyard. The occasional quiet message to North Korea could menace all U.S. policy in the Koreas. And of course, there is still the Red Army. It might be a shadow of its former self, but so are its potential European opponents.

All of these actions have side effects. The U.S. presence in Afghanistan limits Islamist activities in Russia proper. India is no longer a Cold War client; it is an independent power with its own ambitions which might soon involve a partnership with the United States. Excessive weapons sales to China could end with those weapons being used in support of an invasion of the Russian Far East. Large-scale weapons sales to Latin America require Latin American cash to underwrite them. Russian meddling in North Korea would damage relations with China, Japan and South Korea as well as the West. And a Russian military threat against Europe, if it could be mustered, would still face the U.S. nuclear umbrella.

Such actions would also have consequences. The West might often—and vigorously—disagree within itself, but there has not been a Western war in nearly three generations. The West still tends to see Russia as the dangerous "other," and by design or coincidence, Western policy toward the former Soviet Union focuses on rolling back Russian influence, with Ukraine serving as only the most recent example. Russian efforts to push back—even in what is perceived as self-defense— would only provoke a concerted, if not unified, response along Russia's entire economic, political and geographic periphery.

Russia still might have options, but it did lose the Cold War and has fallen in stature massively. In the years since the Cold War, Western options—and strength—have only expanded. Even if Russian efforts were so successful that they deflected all foreign attention from it, Russia would still be doomed. Russia has degraded too far; simply buying time is not enough. . . .

Option 3: Regenerate from Within

Unlike the United States, which has embraced change as part of daily life, Russia is an earthquake society. It does not evolve. Pressures—social, political, economic—build up within the country until it suffers a massive, cataclysmic breakdown and then revival. It is not pleasant; often as a result of Russia's spasms, millions of people die, and not always are they all Russian. But in the rare instances when Russia does change, this is invariably how it happens.

Ironically, the strength of the Soviet period has denied Russia the possibility of foreign events triggering such a change. Russia, as the Union of Soviet Socialist Republics' successor state, has nuclear weapons capable of reaching any point on the globe. As such, a land invasion of Russia is unthinkable.

That simple fact rules out a scenario such as what happened after World War I. Massive defeat by the Central Powers might have triggered the Bolshevik Revolution, but that did not directly result in the constitution of the Soviet Union. Forging Russia into a new entity took another invasion on multiple fronts. Foreign sponsorship of the White [royalist] armies during Russia's civil war—and the direct involvement of hundreds of thousands of foreign troops—was necessary to instill a sense of besiegement sufficient to make the Russians fight back and create a new country. The "mere" loss of Ukraine during World War I was simply not enough. Russia did not merely need to be defeated, humiliated and parsed— Russia itself, not simply Ukraine, had to be directly occupied.

As long as Russia has nukes, that cannot happen.

If Russia is to choose this third path, it must trigger its reformation by itself from wholly domestic developments.

Perhaps it could be done by some sort of natural catastrophe, but to be effective the catastrophe would need to be sufficient to mobilize the entire Russian population. Russian society's muted response to the Beslan massacre—in which Chechen militants killed 350 Russian citizens, half of them children—indicates that terrorism will not be a sufficient stimulus. Depopulation caused by HIV might prove a trigger, but by the time the effects are obvious, there would not be much of a Russia left to revive.

Someone Other Than Putin Is Needed

That leaves the personal touch of a Russian leader to shake the state to its very core.

Most likely, Putin is not the man for the job. He is, among all else, from St. Petersburg. He sees Russia's future in the

West, particularly the European West—but only on Russia's terms. Of course, this is not how realignment of civilizations works. Ask the Spanish (who took a leave of absence from the West during the Franco years [1939–1975]), or the Greeks (who have shuttled between West and East), or the Poles (forced separation), or the Romanians (never really in the West) or the Turks (wanting, but not too desperately, to join), or—in a few years—the Ukrainians (who really have no idea what they are signing up for). To join the West you must change; the West does not change to join you.

Putin also is a gradualist. Russia cannot even attempt the necessary internal renaissance until such time as the oligarchs are liquidated—not merely reshuffled, as is happening currently. That necessitates a Russian upheaval on a scale for which Putin does not appear to have the stomach. Putin has been in command for four years, and in that time he has liquidated four oligarchs: Boris Berezovsky, Vladimir Gusinsky, Rem Vyakhirev and Mikhail Khodorkovsky.

Four oligarchs in four years. Not exactly revolutionary.

Making matters worse, all the assets of these four have either been expropriated to other private oligarchs or shuffled into the hands of a growing class of state oligarchs such as [Russia's giant natural gas company] Gazprom CEO Alexei Miller.

Actually eliminating the oligarchs as a class (which, incidentally, controls nearly 70 percent of the country's economy) will require a massive national spasm complete with a complete scrapping and reformation of the country's legal structure, up to and including the constitution. Investors who have been spooked by Russia's anti-oligarchic efforts have not seen anything yet.

But just because Putin is not the spy for the job does not mean Russia is not capable. Russian leaders have done this before. Peter the Great did it. Ivan the Terrible did it. Joseph Stalin did it. It tends not to be pretty.

> "It is likely that undetected smuggling has occurred, and we are concerned about the total amount of [weapons-usable nuclear] material that could have been diverted."

Russia's Unsafe Nuclear Stockpile Is a Threat to Global Stability

National Intelligence Council

In the following viewpoint, the National Intelligence Council (NIC) argues that both military storage facilities and civilian nuclear power plants in Russia are inadequately guarded and maintained, and thus vulnerable to theft of nuclear material and terrorist attack. The NIC produces "estimative" intelligence—forward-looking assessments of national security issues, drawing on expertise inside and outside of government—for the CIA and senior U.S. policymakers. Its best-known reports are National Intelligence Estimates (NIEs), classified briefs that discuss likely five- to fifteen-year scenarios, such as prospects for stability in U.S.-occupied Iraq. The following is taken from an unclassified report to .Congress, the NIC's most recent assessment of the safety and security of Russian nuclear facilities.

National Intelligence Council, "Annual Report to Congress on the Safety and Security of Russian Nuclear Facilities and Military Forces," April 2006, www.dni.gov.

As you read, consider the following questions:

1. According to Russian officials cited by the author, how many nuclear warheads from the former Soviet stockpile have been dismantled, and what happened to the rest of the nuclear weapons in former Soviet Union territories?

2. What examples does the NIC give of documented thefts of weapons-usable nuclear materials between 1991 and 2003?

3. According to the NIC, what is the most notable flaw in the design of Russian nuclear reactors?

We are concerned that Russia may not sustain U.S.-provided security upgrades of facilities over the long-term given the cost and technical sophistication of some of the equipment involved. . . .

Since the dissolution of the Soviet Union, Moscow has consolidated the former Soviet stockpile into storage sites in Russia. Russian officials have stated that thousands of nuclear warheads from the former Soviet stockpile have been dismantled since 1991; over 10,000 warheads reportedly have been eliminated. Moscow relies on nuclear weapons as its primary means of deterrence, however, and will continue to have thousands of nuclear warheads in its inventory for the foreseeable future. . . .

Who Is Responsible for Nuclear Stockpile Security?

The 12th GUMO [part of the Russian Defense Ministry] is responsible for the physical protection and safety of nuclear weapons. Specialists from the 12th GUMO carry out all maintenance work in close collaboration with the warhead designers. The 12th GUMO also is responsible for nuclear warhead shipments throughout Russia.

- All nuclear weapons storage sites, except those subordinate to the strategic missile troops, fall under the 12th GUMO's responsibility, thus facilitating a uniform policy in matters of operation and physical security.

- In peacetime all nuclear munitions except those on ICBMs and SLBMs [intercontinental and submarine-launched ballistic missiles] in alert status are stored in nuclear weapons storage sites. ·

- The Russians employ a multi-layered approach that includes physical, procedural, and technical measures to secure their weapons.

Since the September 2001 terrorist attacks in the United States, President [Vladimir] Putin and other Russian officials have conducted a public campaign to provide assurances that terrorists have not acquired Russian nuclear weapons or material.

- In October 2002, former Minister of Atomic Energy [Yevgeny] Adamov stated, "Neither [Osama] Bin Ladin nor anyone else could steal a nuclear weapon from anywhere in the former Soviet Union. During my time as minister, I carried out a comprehensive stock-taking of everything we had and had had, and traced the history of all the warheads ever produced. So, everything there was on the territories of the former USSR [Soviet Union] republics was returned to Russia. . . . Nothing was stolen from us. So, neither Bin Ladin, nor Iraq nor Iran could make use of these explosive devices."

- In a September 2006 interview, 12th GUMO chief Vladimir Verkhovtsev enumerated the technical improvements and modernization efforts at Russian warhead sites, concluding that "On the whole, the state of security and protection of the Russian Ministry of Defense nuclear weapons storage bases provides reliable security of nuclear munitions."

Contradictory Reports About Attempted Thefts

Russian officials previously reported that terrorists have targeted Russian nuclear weapon storage sites. According to then-chief of the 12th GUMO [Igor] Valynkin, Russian authorities twice (in 2002 and 2003) thwarted efforts to gain access to nuclear weapon storage sites in the European part of Russia.

- In December 2005, however, Valynkin declared that there have been no attempts to enter Russian nuclear weapons storage facilities, adding "theft or leakage of arms from our facilities is impossible."

Weapons-usable material includes uranium enriched to 20 percent or greater in the uranium-235 or uranium-233 isotopes (highly enriched uranium—HEU) and any plutonium containing less than 80 percent of the isotope plutonium-238.

Weapons-grade material is typically defined as uranium enriched to about 90 percent or greater uranium-235 or uranium-233, or plutonium containing about 90 percent or greater plutonium-239.

Nuclear Materials Are Vulnerable

Russian facilities housing weapons-usable nuclear material vary from small research facilities and fuel cycle facilities to those involved with nuclear weapons research, development, and production.

Small research facilities, although typically underfunded, usually have smaller, static inventories of weapons-usable nuclear material and are easier to secure. Large fuel cycle facilities have larger, varying inventories that are more difficult to account for and much harder to secure.

The United States seeks to complete material protection, control, and accounting (MPC&A) upgrades at Russia's nuclear material facilities by 2008. With U.S. assistance,

International Community Unsure of Safety Measures

David Albright at the Washington-based Institute for Science and International Security says Moscow has a massive nuclear stockpile.

"We would estimate," he says "that the total stock of plutonium and highly enriched uranium in Russia that we're worried about is about 1,280 tons. You know, a relatively few kilograms—four or five kilograms of plutonium [or] 15 to 20 kilograms of highly enriched uranium—this is enough for a nuclear weapon." . . .

The Cooperative Threat Reduction program has spent $400 million building the massive "Mayak" repository for nuclear warheads and materials near the Russian city of Ozersk. It was completed in December 2003, and features walls 7 meters thick built to withstand bombs, shellfire and other types of attacks. But it remain[ed] empty [until July 2006, and disagreement over international inspections continues].

Voice of America,
"How Secure Is Russia's Nuclear Stockpile?" November 17, 2005.

Russia's MPC&A practices have been slowly improving over the last several years, but risks of undetected theft remain.

- Counterintelligence concerns that have led Russia to prevent direct U.S. access to sensitive materials has impeded U.S. efforts to improve the security of Rosatom's [state agency for atomic energy] nuclear weapons complex, where significant quantities of material are stored.

- Ministry of Internal Affairs (MVD) guards at Russian nuclear facilities have displayed vulnerabilities to discipline problems common to other Russian military units, including hazing, accidental shootings and suicides.

- An April 2006 [Russian] Federal Service for Environmental, Technological, and Nuclear Oversight report expressed concern at the number of minor safety violations at nuclear facilities in 2005, but concluded that nuclear safety had improved overall.

In November 2002, Yuri Vishnevskiy, then head of Gosatomnadzor [nuclear regulatory agency], told a news conference that there have been documented instances of nuclear materials, including grams of weapons-grade uranium, disappearing from Russian nuclear materials processing facilities. At the time, [Alexander] Rumyantsev, then head of Rosatom, acknowledged the missing material but claimed that, "Everything that was lost was subsequently traced and returned to the relevant arsenals."

- We assess that it is unlikely that Russian authorities or other governments would have been able to recover all the material likely stolen.

- In March 2005, Rumyantsev said that there have been no cases of theft of fissile materials from Russia's nuclear facilities, seemingly contradicting earlier statements.

Detected Diversions

Russian institutes have lost weapons-usable nuclear materials in thefts in amounts greater than a few milligrams. In each known case, government authorities eventually seized the diverted material. For example:

- In 1992, 1.5 kilograms of 90-percent-enriched weapons-grade uranium were stolen from the Luch Production Association.

- In 1994, approximately 3.0 kilograms of 90-percent-enriched weapons-grade uranium were stolen in Moscow.

- In 1999, the U.S. government confirmed a seizure of weapons-usable nuclear material in Bulgaria. The material—approximately four grams of HEU—probably originated in Russia.

- In 2003, a Russian/Armenian citizen carrying approximately 160 grams of HEU was arrested on Georgian territory. The origin of the material is being investigated.

There have been other press reports about materials seized in Russia about which we have no further information because Russia typically does not reveal the results of its investigations. Press reports generally overstate the impact of stolen material, often incorrectly referring to or implying that depleted, natural, or low-enriched uranium are weapons-usable material.

The number of seizures of stolen material and reported theft attempts over the last several years has declined, apparently as a result of several possible factors: U.S. assistance to improve security at Russian facilities, a possible decrease in smuggling, or smugglers becoming more knowledgeable about evading detection. Nevertheless, it is likely that undetected smuggling has occurred, and we are concerned about the total amount of material that could have been diverted over the last 15 years.

Safety and Security at Russian Civilian Nuclear Power Plants

Rosatom has announced ambitious plans to begin construction of new reactors with enhanced safety features. In July 2006, the Russian government adopted the concept for a Federal Targeted Program aimed at the development of Russia's nuclear energy industry complex through 2015, which would provide approximately 25 billion dollars for domestic nuclear expansion. The proposed program would bring 10 new reactors on line by 2016 with two additional reactors commissioned each year thereafter.

Western assistance has been improving the safety systems and operating procedures at Soviet-designed nuclear reactors. However, inherent design deficiencies in RBMK and older-model WER reactors will prevent them from ever meeting Western safety standards. The most notable design flaw in these reactors is the lack of a Western-style containment structure to prevent the release of fission products in the event of a serious accident.

Rosatom head [Sergei] Kiryenko stated in July 2006 that all Russian nuclear power plants are safely guarded by military and technical means. He added that Rosatom had conducted 364 training exercises in 2005, including antiterrorist drills. Even with increased security, however, Russian nuclear power plants—like those in many countries—almost certainly will remain vulnerable to a well-planned and -executed terrorist attack, which could cause significant damage or even a radiological release.

> *"There is no doubt that security for Russia's nuclear warheads and materials has in fact improved substantially over the last dozen years."*

Russia Has Made Some Progress in Securing Its Nuclear Stockpile

Matthew Bunn and Anthony Wier

In the following viewpoint, Matthew Bunn and Anthony Wier maintain that Russia has made substantial progress in locking down its nuclear stockpile since the early 1990s, including the recovery of highly enriched uranium (HEU) from other former Soviet states. In the past they have argued that post-Soviet Russia is dangerously vulnerable to nuclear theft and smuggling, but here Bunn and Wier credit U.S.-Russian cooperation for improvements in storage facilities, better security at nuclear sites, and accounting for nuclear material. These upgrades are "sufficient to protect against modest groups of armed outsiders, or one to two insiders, or both together"—not secure enough in light of existing terrorist and criminal threats, the authors warn, but better than security levels in some other countries. Matthew

Bunn is a senior research associate and Anthony Wier is a research associate at Harvard University's John F. Kennedy School of Government.

As you read, consider the following questions:

1. What do the authors describe as the most egregious nuclear security weaknesses of the 1990s?

2. According to Bunn and Wier, comprehensive upgrades have been completed in what percentage of buildings with weapons-grade nuclear material in the entire former Soviet Union? What other "rapid upgrades" have been completed at additional nuclear sites?

3. In the authors' view, what did the 2005 Bratislava nuclear security summit achieve?

There is no doubt that security for Russia's nuclear warheads and materials has in fact improved substantially over the last dozen years. Russia's economy has stabilized, and has been growing steadily since 1998. Nuclear experts and workers are now paid a living wage, on time, reducing the incentives to steal, and the electricity for nuclear security systems is no longer being shut off for non-payment of bills. Moreover, the Russian security services are more pervasive than they were a decade ago, including at nuclear sites. The most egregious nuclear security weaknesses of the early 1990s—gaping holes in fences, buildings with no detector at the door to sound an alarm if someone was carrying out plutonium—have largely been fixed, even at sites where U.S.-funded security upgrades have not been completed. It is unlikely that there are any remaining facilities in Russia that are not adequately protected against the minimal theft threats that succeeded in the mid-1990s—a single outsider walking through a gaping hole in a fence, snapping a padlock on a shed, stealing HEU [highly enriched uranium], and retracing his steps without being noticed for hours, or a single insider with no particular plan repeatedly removing small amounts of

HEU and walking out without detection. But the threat of nuclear theft remains substantial, as even the upgraded security systems being installed with U.S. assistance are unlikely to be able to defend against the huge threats terrorists and criminals have shown they can pose in today's Russia.

Much of the improvement in Russia's nuclear security system has come as a result of cooperation between the United States and Russia. . . . U.S.-funded comprehensive upgrades have been completed for 54% of the buildings with weapons-usable nuclear material in the former Soviet Union (including all of the buildings in the non-Russian states). Rapid upgrades, such as bricking over windows and installing nuclear material detectors at exits, have been completed for a modest number of additional nuclear material buildings and a substantial number of additional warhead sites. Upgrades at warhead sites have gotten a slower start, but are catching up: those upgrades the two sides considered to be needed (comprehensive upgrades at most permanent warhead sites, only rapid upgrades at some temporary sites) had been completed for 48 warhead sites, which we estimate represents some 40% of the total number of sites, as of the end of . . . 2005.

At the same time, Russia has continued to take steps to strengthen nuclear security on its own—though these appear to be only limited initial steps toward putting in place the security measures that are needed to meet today's threats. Over the past year, the Rosatom [the Russian federal nuclear power agency] continued a series of in-depth inspections of physical protection and nuclear material accounting at Rosatom sites (launched with U.S. funding), uncovering a wide range of problems and weaknesses which the inspection teams then began to help sites address. The Russian government completed a new basic regulation on nuclear security, which will take a more graded approach to protecting different types of nuclear materials, and will for the first time require facilities to have defenses adequate to protect against an identified design basis threat (DBT)—though as of the spring of 2006, the new rules were not yet issued. Russia announced new budget allocations for nuclear safety and security, but little public information on specific spending for security was made available. Finally, a number of sites invested in improved security measures themselves, to comply with Russian regulations.

Progress Since Bratislava

The accord on nuclear security reached at the February 2005 summit in Bratislava, Slovakia, between U.S. President George [W.] Bush and Russian President Vladimir Putin has led to a significant acceleration of U.S.-Russian nuclear security cooperation, and heightened the dialogue on key subjects such as security culture and plans for sustaining security upgrades. The inter-agency process the summit established, under Secretary of Energy Samuel Bodman and his Russian counterpart (first Alexander Rumiantsev and [then] Sergei Kirienko) has helped push progress toward completing agreed milestones. Soon after the Bratislava summit, Russian officials provided a list of additional nuclear warhead sites where they would permit security cooperation. By June 2005, in the bilateral group's first progress report to President Bush and President Putin, the two sides had reached agreement on a joint plan to complete agreed sets of nuclear security upgrades at an agreed list of nuclear warhead and nuclear material sites by the end of 2008—though some nuclear material and nuclear warhead sites are not yet on the agreed list.

Russia also agreed to permit the access the United States believed was needed to implement cooperative security upgrades at a wider range of nuclear warhead sites, and similar access has now been worked out for nearly all of the buildings containing weapons-usable nuclear material in Russia. Key exceptions to these access arrangements, however, are Russia's two remaining nuclear weapons assembly and disassembly fa-

U.S.-Russian Cooperation

"Working together, Russia and the United States will each convert 34 metric tons of weapons-grade plutonium into fuel for use in civilian nuclear power plants. The United States has also purchased more than 300 metric tons of Russian highly-enriched uranium, and blended it down for use as fuel in civilian nuclear reactors. Many of you know that about 20 percent of U.S. electricity is generated by nuclear power. Yet you may not know that half of that figure is generated using the highly-enriched uranium purchased from Russia. So about one in ten light bulbs in America is powered by nuclear material from weapons that used to be aimed at our country.

"Other joint efforts with Russia to better secure and safeguard nuclear weapons and nuclear materials are delivering results as well. Through the Nunn-Lugar Cooperative Threat Reduction program, we are working with Russia to make possible secure transportation of nuclear warheads removed from delivery systems, to improve security at nuclear weapon storage and dismantlement facilities, and to eliminate retired delivery systems like missiles and bombers.

"And through the Bratislava Initiative, our two nations are working together to upgrade security at Russian nuclear weapons storage sites and nuclear material storage facilities. The United States Department of Energy has completed work at 85 percent of the sites identified under this initiative, and is on schedule to complete work at all the identified sites by December 2008."

National security advisor Stephen Hadley, remarks to the Center for International Security and Cooperation, Stanford University, February 8, 2008. www.whitehouse.gov.

cilities (known in Russia as the "serial production enterprises"). So far, those two sites remain too sensitive to allow cooperation to move forward, though Rosatom's security chief visited the comparable U.S. facility at Pantex [in Texas] in late 2004. The two sides continue to discuss cooperative approaches to upgrading these facilities without compromising nuclear secrets.

In September 2005, as called for at Bratislava, the two sides held in-depth workshops on strengthening security culture and on best practices in securing and accounting for nuclear material, bringing the dialogue on those topics to a new level, and discussions of both issues are ongoing. During 2005, the two sides also began drafting a joint plan for sustaining nuclear security after international assistance phases out, with an explicit understanding that Russian funding would have to increase as external funding declines. In addition, after Bratislava, Russia and the United States agreed on a joint plan for returning Soviet-supplied HEU to Russia by the end of 2010 (though under current plans, a significant portion of that HEU will be addressed outside of Russia, a job that is expected to extend beyond 2010). . . .

Locking Down Nuclear Stockpiles in the Former Soviet States Outside Russia

In those former Soviet states other than Russia that inherited weapons-usable nuclear material, U.S.-funded security and accounting upgrades were completed in the late 1990s, though some further improvements have been made since then. As in Russia, it is unlikely that a single outsider or a single low-level insider could any longer steal nuclear material without detection from any of these facilities. The three questions asked about Russia, however—are the upgrades enough to meet today's threats, are human operators using the upgraded systems correctly and taking security seriously, and will high security be sustained—all apply here as well. Indeed, the question of the adequacy of upgraded security systems is particularly troubling here, as these facilities have only been upgraded to meet rather vague International Atomic Energy Agency (IAEA) recommendations—a security standard significantly lower than the upgrades being implemented in Russia are designed to meet. . . .

At the Institute of Nuclear Physics in Uzbekistan, for instance, the DOE [U.S. Department of Energy] declared that it had completed upgrades in 1996. It then did so again in 2000, when further upgrades were implemented to meet revised IAEA recommendations. Yet given the presence in Uzbekistan of an armed Islamic movement closely linked to al Qaeda, and the political unrest that resulted in the government's brutal clampdown in Andijon, the capital, in May 2005, this facility remained a top priority for removing the HEU entirely. Fresh HEU fuel was in fact removed from the facility in September 2004, and DOE completed sending back to Russia a large stockpile of irradiated HEU fuel from this facility in April 2006. The shipment of irradiated HEU from Uzbekistan, in particular, represented a major milestone in the effort to send Soviet-supplied HEU back to Russia, finally getting past the bureaucratic obstacles to implementing such shipments under the terms of Russia's spent fuel import law that had delayed the effort for years.

Also in 2006, a cache of 2.5 kilograms of fresh HEU was returned to Russia from Latvia, and discussions continued with Belarus, Ukraine, and Kazakhstan about returning their HEU stocks to Russia or blending them down. Perhaps most impressive, Kazakhstan blended down some 2.9 tons of HEU left over from its closed Aqtau breeder reactor, in a private-government partnership financed in part by the Nuclear Threat Initiative. This operation eliminated the danger that this material could ever be used in bombs without complex re-enrichment.

Periodical Bibliography

The following articles have been selected to supplement the diverse views presented in this chapter.

Neil Buckley — "Across Putin's Russia," (slideshow with audio), *Financial Times.com*, February 17, 2008. www.ft.com/indepth/russianelections.

Economist — "Trouble in the Pipeline," May 8, 2008.

Anatle Kaletsky — "No Wonder Russia Is Paranoid," *Times* (London) *Online*, April 3, 2008. www.timesonline.co.uk./tol/comment/columnists/anatole_kaletsky/article3670814.ece.

Ivan Krastev — "What Russia Wants," *Foreign Policy*, May–June 2008.

NATO — "NATO-Russia Relations: Building a Lasting and Inclusive Peace in the Euro-Atlantic Area," *North Atlantic Treaty Organization*, May 14, 2008. www.nato.int/issues/nato-russia/topic.html.

Vladimir Putin — "Putin Q&A: Full Transcript," *Time*, December 18, 2007.

Israel Rafalovich — "Between Antagonism and Ambivalence: Russia-China Relations," *Thought Leader, Mail & Guardian Online*, March 24, 2008. www.thoughtleader.co.za/israelrafalovich/2008/03/24/between-antagonism-and-ambivalence-russia-china-relations.

Dmitri Trenin — "Russia's Threat Perception and Strategic Posture," U.S. Army Strategic Studies Institute, November 2007. www.StrategicStudiesInstitute.army.mil.

Richard Weitz — "U.S.-Russia Accord Could Facilitate Nonproliferation, Civil Nuclear Cooperation," *World Politics Review*, May 12, 2008.

CHAPTER 2

Is Russia Moving
Toward Democracy?

Chapter Preface

In 2002, following a wave of violent incidents targeting foreigners and racial and ethnic minorities in major cities, the Russian parliament passed a law against "extremism" that, in a BBC (British Broadcasting Corporation) analysis, defined as extremist "any attempt to forcibly change the Russian constitution, undermine the country's security, take over authority by force, or carry out terrorist activities. It also allows the police to disband parties and movements which have been identified as extremist." Much like the USA PATRIOT Act that followed the 9/11 attacks, a law that broadened the authority of law enforcement agencies, the Russian extremism law has been controversial. Critics charge that it violates civil rights and is worded vaguely to allow the government to clamp down not on racism and ultranationalism but on opposition parties, the media, and religious or human rights organizations. The BBC points out that this law allows the courts to "hand down severe punishments for demonstrators at unsanctioned protests." Supporters in and out of the Kremlin defended the 2002 law, however, as a necessary tool to curb racial violence and pro-terrorist sentiment and to increase national security.

The extremism law became even more controversial in 2007, when it was twice beefed up by expanding the definition of extremism to include, for example, "slandering an official of the Russian Federation." Printers and publishers can be fined for distributing extremist literature and people suspected of extremism are barred from running for public office. Now, critics warn, it's clear that the extremism law is meant to intimidate the media and stifle opposition to Kremlin policy; if extremism is now whatever the government says it is, any person risks arrest and any organization can be shut down for virtually anything it says or does.

The Kremlin, and pro-Kremlin parties such as the United Russia Party (Russia's largest political party), insist that this criticism is unfounded and stricter laws are necessary. According to Oleg Morozov, deputy speaker of the legislature called the Duma, "The enemies of Russia are attempting to use Russia as a trigger for explosive ethnic conflicts designed to destabilize society and cause the disintegration of the country. We need to establish zero tolerance in our society for xenophobia, nationalism, and extremism in all its forms." Indeed, there have been public complaints that the Kremlin hasn't done enough to punish and prevent hate crimes against migrants from former Soviet Central Asia.

There is evidence, however, to back up critics' claims. In 2007 the government began proceedings to shut down the liberal Yabloko party for distributing two books by liberal intellectual Andrei Piontkovsky that criticized the Kremlin. The National Bolshevik Party has been banned on the grounds that its leftist ideology constitutes extremism. Radio and TV stations have cut their live debate and talk shows because any speech deemed extremist during a broadcast is reason for the authorities to shut the station down. Retired truck driver Pyotr Gagarin, age seventy-one, faced criminal prosecution (and a possible three-year prison sentence) for calling the governor of his province a "liar" and "scum" at a local gathering to protest high food prices and job loss.

The viewpoints in the following chapter consider whether recent legislation and judicial action represent legitimate exercise of authority or undemocratic abuse of power, and the larger question of whether the democratization movement that followed the breakup of the Soviet Union has stalled in Russia.

> *"The distance Russia has traveled in a democratic direction . . . is going more slowly than many . . . had hoped; but it is moving more swiftly than I had expected."*

Russia Is Moving Toward Democracy

Vyacheslav Nikonov

In the following viewpoint, Vyacheslav Nikonov argues that Russian political institutions and Vladimir Putin's leadership style may not fit Western ideas of democracy, but there is plenty of evidence of a strong democratic process in Russia today. Westerners have to understand that Russians reject both the authoritarianism of communism and the anything-goes chaos of former president Boris Yeltsin's early post-Soviet reforms, when "practically nobody was running the country." In the new Russia, he maintains, the power of corrupt oligarchs has been reduced, the judicial system has become more independent, more than thirty political parties are free to field candidates for elected office, and freedom of speech is greater than in any other country in the world. Vyacheslav Nikonov is president of the Polity Foundation,

Vyacheslav Nikonov, "The Paradoxes of Russian Democracy," *Carnegie Reporter,* vol. 2, Spring 2003. Copyright © 2003 Carnegie Corporation of New York. Reproduced by permission of Carnegie Corporation of New York.

a nongovernmental research and consulting group founded in 1993 to promote political and economic reform—specifically, the creation of a civil society and a law-based state—in Russia.

As you read, consider the following questions:

1. What went wrong with Boris Yeltsin's democratic strategy, and how did Vladimir Putin put democratization back on track, according to the author?

2. The Russian government, like the U.S. government, is divided into executive, legislative, and judicial branches. According to Nikonov, how does the Russian president's role differ from the American head of state's?

3. Nikonov argues that the Russian people lack faith in "the sanctity and stability of basic democratic values." In his view, why are the majority of Russians indifferent to the concept of democracy?

Russia launched an attempt to break free from authoritarianism in the late 1980s and early 1990s, when the collapse of the USSR [Soviet Union] gave rise to hopes of a quick and painless transformation to a genuinely democratic country with a flourishing market economy, entering into the family of civilized countries. That period was dominated by undivided criticism with regard to the past, and the western model of democracy was perceived as the absolute standard.

To what extent has the democratic breakthrough been successful? Many western journalists and Russian rights activists give this response: Boris Yeltsin [president of Russia from 1991 to 1999] made heroic efforts to lay the foundations of a genuine democratic regime, and Vladimir Putin [Yeltzin's successor] made several steps backwards—towards a controlled democracy.

I have a hard time accepting this characterization, and not only because I am unaware of any examples of uncontrolled democracy. It is just that the Russian democratic process is developing in a much more complex, paradoxical manner.

The Basics of Russia's Constitutional Government

During Yeltsin's regime, anarchy reigned because practically nobody was running the country and it was in a state of free fall. Yes, there was democracy, insofar as there were free elections for the offices established by the Constitution, but there were also elements of authoritarianism, despotism and oligarchy, as we see from the fact that during Yeltsin's prolonged absences, the country was often run by a collection of his relatives, better known as the Family. This group also included powerful tycoons, who made up a new financial elite.

Putin, on the other hand, has been able to restore some order to the country and reduce anarchy. His family does not run the country. Oligarchy is not at the helm. At the same time, there have not been any radical changes to the elections. The Constitution has stayed the same.

Does democracy offer a division of power, a system of checks and balances? I believe they are not superfluous, although in the European countries the division of power is almost unheard of, and this does not prevent them from being generally democratic. The Russian constitutional system is a major improvement compared to the Communist system, founded on Vladimir Lenin's ideas of the merging of the executive and legislative powers and the subordination of the courts to the control of the Communist Party. The division of powers in the current Constitution is mandated at one point, but it is effectively refuted by other articles. The reason is that the president, invested with enormous authority, is outside the system of checks and balances, and is not a part of the executive branch (this branch is represented by the cabinet of ministers). At the same time, the head of state effectively fulfills the functions of both the executive and the legislative powers through his authority to issue edicts.

Yeltsin dealt with an independent and sharply opposed parliament, which was dominated by Communists and nationalists who did not allow a single democratic law to be adopted. Now, thanks to strenuous efforts by the Kremlin, Putin has a majority, which allows him to adopt almost any reform laws against the objections of the Communist and nationalist opposition, whose size has been significantly reduced.

The judicial system has escaped from the control of one party and has become formally independent. However, judges' salaries remain low, which has made the judiciary accessible to the trends of the material world. Today, the role of the courts is growing, but this is due in large part to the fact that Russia's "entrepreneurs" have finally grown tired of clarifying issues with the help of hired killers and have turned, instead, to the courts.

Unique Russian Circumstances

If we were to judge by the criteria of political pluralism and freedom of activity of political parties, Russia would appear to be the most democratic country in the world. There have never been fewer than thirty parties on the ballot for the State Duma [parliament], and hundreds of others have been allowed to register and participate in the primary elections. The menu is enormous, but the quality of the political cuisine leaves something to be desired. And to complicate matters, the highest authorities are not generally associated with any party. Not surprisingly, party loyalties have not sprung up; no more than 1.5 percent of voters associate themselves firmly with a particular party, and people perceive the struggle between the parties as a largely unnecessary and annoying farce.

The important factors for democracy are a local initiative, a vertical distribution of power and federalism. Russia, of course, is a federation to a much greater degree than the Soviet Union was. Governors in the 89 divisions of the federation are elected by a national vote, in which the elections are not simultaneous, and therefore the country remains in a condition of permanent election campaigning in the various regions. As early as the beginning of the 1990s, Yeltsin proposed that the governors take as much sovereignty as they could swallow. They swallowed a lot. The power was in the hands of 89 powerful elected leaders, among whom there were almost no reformers or even honest and competent people. They were completely independent and outside the control of the Kremlin, which was much more democratic than the regional lords. Local initiative came under repression from the opposition, the free press and the arbitrary redistribution of property. All the governors adopted laws for themselves, which did not prevent a quarter of the normative [prescriptive] acts passed in the regions from contradicting the federal laws and the Constitution.

Putin is not giving out sovereignty; he is taking it back. The president has theoretically been granted the right to remove a governor from office for violating the Constitution, although this right has not yet been exercised. Representatives of the president in seven federal regions, by one means or another, have made sure that the local laws do not contradict the Constitution. The reform-minded Kremlin has achieved greater control over the regional authorities, which are still very anti-reform. I will not presume to say which system— Yeltsin's or Putin's—is more in line with the interests of the democratic process.

Growing Freedoms

Freedom of private enterprise has appeared in Russia. The activity that was punishable by a prison sentence in the Soviet Union has become a respectable business. A compelling game took place in the 1990s, one that the American robber barons did not even dream of: an enormous country, where everything—from the electrical plants down to the nails—was owned by the state, [and] was passing into private hands. Democracy had very little to do with all this. The winners of the game were those who were able to convince government offi-

Russian Blogging: "A Vital Democratic Spirit in the Raw"

Social justice [in Russia] is on the forward march. [The actions of Russian bloggers who spread the word to fight a corrupt drug company in 2007 shows the] ... roles that blogging can play in a country as complex, if not outright Byzantine, as Russia.

Among the biggest positives, which still outweigh the negatives at this point, is the emergence of a fresh and networked public sphere that is so badly needed in Russia. ...

In fact, the blog post touched off a mini Russian revolution. It's hard to remember a time when a program on Russian TV or an article in a Russian newspaper did the same. Most of them today are, at best, just dull—and have little of the vitality and vigor of the discussions that are happening online.

As far as Russia's future is concerned, and the pervasive questions about its democratic path, the networked aspect of this public sphere may be the most important of all considerations. It has the potential for fostering greater social and political change in the country.

Evgeny Morozov,
"Welcome to Russian Consumer Democracy,"
Globalist, *October 23, 2007.*

cials, through bribes and corruption, to make them billionaires rather than someone else. Entrepreneurship became so unrestrained that the "oligarchs" that appeared, having free access to any government office, decided that it was unnecessary, for instance, to pay taxes. Incidentally, the rest of the population didn't do so either.

Putin sent a series of messages to the oligarchs. The first was: federal policy was the president's business. The second was: at least make it look like you're paying taxes. The third was: each of you is subject to investigation. The oligarchs became less independent. Those who did not take the first message seriously were confronted with the implementation of the third.

Freedom of speech has also appeared in the new Russia. Under Yeltsin it was much more abundant than in any other country in the world I know. The concepts of political correctness, reliability of information or moral imperatives never entered the minds of the journalists. Almost all twenty national television channels were among the opposition. In Putin's Russia, the channels formerly belonging to powerful oligarchs have become more loyal. Freedom of speech has diminished: now there is only slightly more of it than in any other country in the world. When one of my American friends asked whether there was opposition in today's Russia, I asked him to give me an example of an opposition television channel in the U.S. After some hesitation, he mentioned Fox News. Compared to Fox News, any Russian channel is the opposition. And the spectrum of opinions represented in the Russian media is several miles broader than anywhere else. Of course, this is not so much a sign of excessive democracy as of a lack of ideological reference points and intellectual confusion.

Paradoxically, Popular Indifference

Democratic regimes are strengthened when their foundations are based on the people's faith in the sanctity and stability of basic democratic values. This is just what is lacking in Russia. The people who demanded democracy in the late 1980s and early 1990s are now indifferent at best. The very concept of democracy, unfortunately, has largely been discredited. It is associated in people's minds with the age of Yeltsinism—the loss of all the safeguards of the Soviet period, a 50-percent drop in the economy, four-digit inflation, a transfer of property to the hands of a few, corruption, a surge in crime, an increase in the cost of living, heating and electricity and the virtual disappearance of free medicine.

According to data by the All-Russian Center for the Study of Public Opinion (VTsIOM), only 15 percent of the population believes that they have gained from the democratic and market reforms, and 73 percent believe that they have lost. Seventy-five percent of those surveyed believe that order is important for Russia, even if instituting certain limitations on personal freedoms are necessary to achieve it.

Still, the Russians do not want to move backwards. By "order" they do not mean a retreat from democratic principles, but rather political and economic stability (46 percent), strict adherence to the laws (35 percent), a stop to the looting of the country (34 percent), and an opportunity for everyone to enjoy their rights (16 percent). People also have a positive view of their initial achievements in freedom of speech, freedom to travel abroad, entrepreneurship, the right to strike, etc. It is only the political parties they actively dislike. People are not at all inclined to give up their freedoms; they are simply tired of the shock effects of ten years of difficult changes.

The West Unjustly Criticizes Russian Politics

Though the establishment of Russian democracy is still on a very winding path, the negative characterization of the situation we are witnessing—the evolution from Yeltsin's pure democracy to Putin's controlled democracy—seems to me to be unjustified. In my opinion, if we can in fact speak of a movement, it would be more accurate to say we have moved from Gorbachev's mild authoritarianism to Yeltsin's total anarchy, which is turning to moderate anarchy. Some people have even begun paying their taxes.

If the movement continues along this trajectory, one consequence may indeed be democracy. But it would hardly be western-style democracy. Strictly speaking, there are no historical precedents, no stimuli for the development of democracy according to western standards, as there are, say, among the countries of Central and Eastern Europe, which were told that in order to be admitted to NATO and the European Union, they must follow certain standards. No one is about to admit Russia to these organizations, so it is relatively free to devise standards of its own.

The distance Russia has traveled in a democratic direction may be assessed in different ways. It is going more slowly than many, including myself, had hoped; but it is moving more swiftly than I had expected a few years ago.

I will make one totally paradoxical conclusion. Considering the existence of a powerful tsarist tradition in Russia, I have no doubt that a popular president will be capable of implementing democratic reforms, even if society will not be very happy about it.

> *"[Russia's] independent media has been all but wiped out, elected regional governors have been replaced with hand-picked Kremlin cronies and most forms of political opposition have been crushed."*

Russia Is Moving Away from Democracy

Peter Wilson

In the following viewpoint, journalist Peter Wilson argues that Putin's eight years in power resulted in a move away from democracy, that the election was a sham, and that Dmitry Medvedev, who at the time of this writing was president-elect, is a puppet of Putin. Wilson believes that Putin continues to hold the real power and continues to force Russia's retreat into authoritarianism. Peter Wilson is Europe correspondent for the daily newspaper The Australian.

As you read, consider the following questions:

1. Why does Wilson call the election of Putin's replacement "a reverse image of the Western understanding of an election?"

2. How is Medvedev's image as a liberal reformer at odds with his actual background and career rise, according to Wilson?

3. According to the author, what percentage of Russians want Putin to remain in power for life?

Olga Kurnosova shakes her head sadly and corrects me when I suggest over lunch in St Petersburg that President Vladimir Putin's candidate is going to win tomorrow's presidential election in Russia.

Yes, the veteran political dissident says, Putin's man Dmitry Medvedev is definitely going to win, with what she guesses will be about 70 percent of the vote. Where I am wrong, though, is in calling it an election. "To be an election there has to be some possibility that the official candidate could actually lose," says Kurnosova, a former MP [member of parliament] in St Petersburg, Putin's home town, who leads the local branch of chess star Garry Kasparov's opposition party Other Russia.

"No, what we are about to have here in Russia is not an election, it is a coronation."

The 2008 "Election" Was a Sham

It certainly does not feel as if there is an election going on in Russia's former imperial capital. There are almost no signs of campaigning: no billboards, posters, television debates or mail-outs clogging letterboxes.

A decade after Boris Yeltsin had to fight hard to win Russia's first fiercely contested presidential election, the campaign to replace his successor, Putin, has been so restrictive and unfair, and the media coverage so biased in favour of the Kremlin's candidate, that the Western election monitoring organisations are not even bothering to send observers.

This shrivelling of democracy in Russia under Putin was neatly illustrated by the precautions Kurnosova took in arranging our interview. A doctor of physics who has known Putin since he and Medvedev began their political careers in the early 1990s as aides to St Petersburg's reformist mayor Anatoly Sobchak, Kurnosova suggested that we meet at a Metro station rather than at her party's office. Constant phone tapping, physical intimidation and ostentatious surveillance by the KGB's [the Soviet Intelligence, secret police and security] successor, the FSB, has forced her party to do as much business as possible away from its own office. "A lot of us have been beaten up and I have been arrested four times, but after a day they generally have to let me out of jail because I have two children," she says in a matter-of-fact way over lunch in a Japanese restaurant.

The selection of Putin's replacement is a reverse image of the Western understanding of an election: that there should be uncertainty before the result is announced but then a clear sense of what direction the new regime will take. In this case there is no doubt that Medvedev, a bland Deputy Prime Minister known only for his career-long loyalty to Putin, will become president but we can only guess about what will happen after that.

Putin Still Holds the Power

The enormously popular Putin, who is stepping down only because of a constitutional limit of two consecutive terms as president, may manage to retain control from his planned new post as prime minister. The former KGB agent is only 55 and is given credit by most Russians for an unprecedented stint of stability and prosperity, even though it is built on a boom in energy prices that has nothing to do with the President.

Putin may prevail on his long-time sidekick to step aside after one term or even sooner to allow him to return to the top job. Or it could all go wrong, with the two men falling out or Putin proving unable to protect his protege from rival factions within the Kremlin.

The headlines on Monday may very well read "A tsar is born," but for at least the short term it is Putin, not the new president, who will be the nation's pre-eminent power. Kurnosova's reference to a coronation sits easily with Russia's obsession with its tumultuous history. Putin is often compared with Ivan the Terrible, the first Russian ruler to call himself tsar or caesar, as the self-styled descendant of the Roman emperor. Ivan centralised power and gave Russia a new confidence in its international standing.

Yet the Russians are also prone to forgetting or denying their past, a tendency that began long before Soviet propaganda artists began airbrushing fallen politicians out of photographs. This trait was personified by another tsar, the False Dmitry. The False Dmitry was an audacious fake who came forward after Ivan's death claiming to be his missing son, who had in fact been assassinated as a child.

The False Dmitry was clearly not who he pretended to be but he won the crown anyway thanks to the gullibility of some of his countrymen and a deliberate decision by others to pretend to believe his lies. His rule lasted only 10 months before he was killed in a palace coup but the episode destabilised Russia for many years.

The False Dmitry's tale . . . comes to mind when considering the public statements . . . of Medvedev, who at 42 is about to become Russia's youngest leader since the days of the tsars. The shy lawyer and bureaucratic fixer has presented himself as a liberal reformer and a democrat with so-called European values. While many other senior figures in Putin's Kremlin are proud to be siloviki, or men of power from the KGB, FSB and the military, Medvedev has highlighted that he is a civilian lawyer who entered politics as a young man working for reform under Anatoly Sobchak [Putin's mentor] and Putin.

Medvedev's Democratic Credentials Are Fake

Medvedev claims that his central goal as president will be the promotion of freedom, including freedom of speech, and he has vowed to strengthen property rights, cut back the bloated state role in the economy and crack down on corruption and the abuse of state powers by bureaucrats and politicians. To that end he says he opposes the present boardroom dominance of government-linked businesses by Kremlin heavies, insisting that he would prefer to see truly independent directors take up those positions.

Even the first False Dmitry would have had a hard time saying all that with a straight face.

Medvedev, after all, holds the juiciest boardroom sinecure, the chairmanship of Gazprom, the world's largest gas company. In that position he has overseen the strong-arming of foreign and Russian firms to force them to hand over lucrative gas assets. Corruption has thrived under the regime in which he is such a senior figure, while the independent media has been all but wiped out, elected regional governors have been replaced by hand-picked Kremlin cronies and most forms of political opposition have been crushed. Mikhail Khodorkovsky, the tycoon who fell out with the Kremlin and began funding opposition MPs, still languishes in jail after a government onslaught in which his oil firm Yukos was grabbed by Moscow, sending a chilling message to other businessmen. Putin's former colleagues from the KGB head the country's oil, media, railways and armaments industries as well as the state airline.

[The March 2008] election will be a new low in post-communist Russian democracy. In 1996 Yeltsin won only 35 percent of the vote in the first round and had to ditch unpopular policies and personnel before winning a two-man run-off with 54 percent of the vote. In 2000, when voters craved a strong leader after Yelstin's mismanagement, Putin managed to win an absolute majority in the first round with 53 percent of the vote. Four years later there was so little competition that he won a hefty 71 percent. He now has so much control that he could hand a similar landslide to virtually anybody he nominated.

That leaves Medvedev's democratic credentials as fake as the electoral process, in which true liberal opponents have been kept out of the race by official pressure and manipulations of electoral laws. Medvedev's opponents [were] Gennady Zyuganov, the veteran communist whose party offers only token criticism of Kremlin policies; ultra-nationalist Vladimir Zhirinovsky, who reliably backs the Kremlin; and Andrei Bogdanov, who claims to be a pro-Europe liberal but constantly praises Putin.

"Opposition" Candidates Are Putin Loyalists

Bogdanov, 38, who is almost unknown, leads the Democratic Party, which won only 90,000 votes in [the December 2007] parliamentary elections, but he has supposedly managed somehow to get the two million signatures required to support a presidential candidacy. He is a former spin doctor for the Kremlin's political party and his campaign is a charade to create the impression of diversity.

As a frontman whose only important credential for the presidency is Putin's endorsement, Medvedev was selected precisely because of his dependence on Putin. His civilian background means he lacks powerful security and KGB networks, leaving him much less likely to build his own power base and shake off Putin's control.

Putin's Russia is a modern version of Vladimir Lenin's one-party state without Karl Marx's economics or Joseph Stalin's [all early shapers of the Soviet Union's history] gulags, but that central control does not mean that all is harmony within the Kremlin. In a fiercely competitive world where se-

Young Russians: "Uneducated About Democracy, Ambivalent About Stalin"

Today, many Russians show symptoms of collective amnesia about the past, and a majority of young Russians believe Joseph Stalin (1929–1953) did more good than bad. . . . As long as they remain positively inclined toward Stalin, young Russians are unlikely to embrace concepts such as justice and human rights. The failure of robust democratic institutions to develop, coupled with a lack of understanding of the past, has left Russians uneducated about democracy, ambivalent about Stalin, and confused about Russia's place in the world. . . .

In 2002–2004, we asked more than 16,500 survey respondents ages 16–64 a question that appears on surveys around the world. Respondents were given three statements and asked which they agreed with most: "Democracy is always preferable," "Authoritarian government is sometimes preferable to democracy," or "The form of government does not matter to people like me." Our results suggest that 34 percent of Russians always prefer democracy, and 33 percent prefer authoritarian rule some of the time; the remaining 33 percent either say it does not matter or decline to answer. In these same surveys, support for democracy is stronger, although far from universal, among the youngest cohort. About 40 percent of 16–29-year-olds always prefer democracy, 29 percent sometimes prefer authoritarian rule, and 31 percent are indifferent or decline to answer.

Sarah E. Mendelson and Theodore P. Gerber,
"Soviet Nostalgia: An Impediment to Russian Democratization,"
Washington Quarterly, *Winter 2005–2006.*

curity service factions keep dossiers of kompromat or compromising material on every prominent figure, anybody can be torn down if they do not have the right sponsors and networks.

The other leading contender for Putin's endorsement during the past two years, Deputy Prime Minister and former KGB agent and defence minister Sergei Ivanov, would have come to office with stronger connections and more anti-Western and authoritarian instincts than Medvedev, but he may also have been harder for Putin to control. While Ivanov, 55, is an old KGB friend of Putin, Medvedev is often described as more like his adopted son. A wooden public speaker who lacks Putin's public confidence and tough charisma, Medvedev has spent 17 years in the shadow of his mentor and owes his entire career to his loyalty to Putin.

Medvedev: Not Leadership Material

Kremlin spin doctors are trying to build up an appealing Medvedev biography but they have uninspiring raw material.

In Putin they had an intriguing character to sell. A working-class kid whose brother died in the Nazi siege of Leningrad, as St Petersburg was then known, Putin was a young hooligan until he became committed to judo. He turned around his life by developing the discipline to go to law school and to pursue his dream of a KGB career, ending up working undercover in what was then East Germany. After working for [Anatoly] Sobchak in the first post-communist government of St Petersburg, Putin was taken to Moscow by Yeltsin and fast-tracked to the top.

Medvedev, on the other hand, was the son of two academics who had an ordinary childhood in Kupchino, a large housing development about 10km south of the [St Petersburg] centre. Designed with plenty of open ground and play areas, it is a characterless stretch of apartment blocks of varying quality put up from the '60s onwards. The stairwell leading to his old apartment has recently been painted, but the rest of the complex has not been renovated for decades.

Teachers at his old school, School 305, do their best to talk up the future president but it is a stretch to make him sound interesting. Dmitry was apparently a nice but unremarkable boy who collected rock music, married Svetlana, the prettiest girl in class, and studied law at St Petersburg State University under future mayor Sobchak. He then worked on Sobchak's first election campaign when the law professor ran for the city council in 1989 against the communist authorities. Putin, who had studied under Sobchak a decade earlier, came on board in 1990.

The following year Sobchak became mayor and Putin was appointed to run the external affairs section of the mayor's office in the grand yellow-painted Smolny Institute, Lenin's old headquarters. Medvedev was his legal adviser. People who knew them both from those days say Putin was "a closed person who was difficult to get to know" but Medvedev was nondescript.

"All I remember is that he was one of the few people in the building shorter than Putin (Medvedev is about 5cm shorter than his mentor) and he made the coffee when I visited," says one male MP from that era who asks not to be named.

When Sobchak's ally in Moscow, Yeltsin, recruited Putin to the Kremlin, he took Medvedev along for the ride, promoting him to a series of top jobs. Sobchak's old campaign office on the posh shopping street Nevksy Prospekt has since been converted into a Museum of the Establishment of Democracy, where curators are scouring their archives of old photos and files for traces of Medvedev.

One photograph that has surfaced in a book on Sobchak, who died in 2000, shows Medvedev at a 2006 memorial gathering, but most of his face is obscured by a guard's shoulder because the photographer did not think he was anybody important. Once a bit pudgy, Medvedev has toned up during the past year and improved his dress sense, often copying Putin's taste for tight woollen jumpers. He combs carefully to cover a thinning hairline and has adopted some of Putin's speech mannerisms, although he is much less likely to stray from a set speech.

"He is not confident enough to have a campaign debate because he simply doesn't have any arguments," says opposition activist Kurnosova, who was a member of the city council when he was an aide. "He would not be able to answer sharp questions, anyone could beat him in a debate. (Russian-born Australian boxer) Kostya Tszyu could beat him and I don't think he (Tszyu) is interested in politics."

The Russian People Are Happier Under Putin's Autocracy

Kurnosova may be a little more scornful than usual because she has just heard that the authorities will not allow her party to hold a march on the day after the election, claiming among other things that the planned route will disrupt tourists at a museum even though the museum is due to be closed. Kurnosova says that all of her party's protests have been peaceful but some of her colleagues feel "if we are going to get arrested anyway it might as well be for something significant."

The remarkable thing about the suppression of the media, opposition parties and independent community groups in this campaign is how unnecessary it all is; even in a fair election Putin's team would still romp home. Putin has achieved little structural reform, infrastructure development or productivity improvements with the enormous windfall from soaring oil and gas prices, but most Russians think he is personally responsible for the commodity-based economic turnaround since 1998, when Russia defaulted on foreign debts and the rouble [or ruble, Russian unit of currency] collapsed. Polls show that more than one-third of Russians want Putin, who is the longest serving leader of the Group of Eight leading industrial nations [G8 includes the United States], to remain in power for life.

Putin's and Medvedev's home town is certainly revelling in the economic recovery, in which the nation's gross domestic product has more than trebled in US dollar terms in the past five years. When I visited 20 years ago, in the dying days of communism, the city felt like an architectural treasure rotting away after 70 years of neglect. The lifts in beautiful canal-side mansions were collapsing through lack of maintenance, the Hermitage museum was leaking and palaces were crumbling. Today, even in winter, the streets are lined with scaffolding for renovations and shops are jammed with products that ordinary Russians could only dream about in the past. Travel agency windows advertise cheap holidays in Egypt and return flights to New York, and new shopping centres are crowded as soon as they are built.

"In the Soviet days we had plenty of money but empty shops, then under Yeltsin there were lots of Western things in the shops but we had no money," says Natalya, a 25-year-old book-keeper relaxing with her husband in an up-market cafe. "Now we can actually buy things. People associate democracy with the '90s when the economy collapsed and we were suddenly living on NATO ration packs. That has made democracy a swearword."

> "If Putin chose to sweep away the con-
> stitution and declare himself a dictator,
> I doubt many Russians would protest."

Russia Is Becoming a Dictatorship

Orlando Figes

In the following viewpoint, Putin critic Orlando Figes argues that during Putin's eight years in office he systematically en-forced an authoritarian political system over a weak Russian civil society, that the 2008 election was a foregone conclusion and Medvedev a puppet, and that Putin will remain in power barely behind the scenes, supported by powerful ex-KGB officials and the resurgence of a pro-strongman sentiment among the Russian people. Orlando Figes is a Russia historian at Birbeck College, University of London.

As you read, consider the following questions:

1. What are the *siloviki*, according to Figes, and how did they squash political opposition in Putin's regime?

2. How are Russia's changing demographics fueling a rising wave of xenophobia and nationalism, in the author's view?

Orlando Figes, "Vlad the Great," *New Statesman,* November 29, 2007. Copyright © 2007 New Statesman, Ltd. Reproduced by permission.

3. According to Figes, how did Putin manage to make ordinary Russians nostalgic for the Soviet Union and even view Stalin in a positive light?

Russia is creeping towards dictatorship. The [2007] parliamentary elections will be another step towards the reestablishment of a one-party system in Russia. No one doubts that the Kremlin-backed United Russia will dominate the next Duma [parliament]—its propaganda dominates the media. To make sure, however, the Electoral Commission has raised the threshold for winning seats from 5 to 7 per cent of the vote and barred many of the weak and divided opposition parties from participating in the poll, using complicated registration laws. Opposition meetings are regularly broken up by the police.

Putinism Is Here to Stay

Vladimir Putin [elected in 2000] may use [his own political party] United Russia's victory to break the constitution by standing for a third term in the presidential elections in March 2008. [Putin did not break the constitution, but supported what many call a puppet regime.] He has spoken ominously of his "moral right" to remain in power. Rallies "For Putin and For Russia" have been organised in a number of towns to encourage him to stand. A more likely scenario, perhaps, is that Putin will simply move from the post of president to that of prime minister, and that a corresponding shift of power will take place; or that he will get one of his cronies elected president ... and replace him when he steps down for reasons of "ill-health". Either way, it doesn't really matter what the outcome of this intrigue is: Putinism is here to stay.

What is Putinism? First, it is a reassertion of the state, a counter-revolution against democracy, which in the eyes of the president's supporters brought Russia to the verge of ruin during the 1990s. The men behind this counter-revolution are the *siloviki* (from the Russian word for power)—men like Putin from the old KGB [the Soviet secret service] (reformed as the FSB), or the armed forces and the "power ministries", which together formed an inner cabinet in Boris Yeltsin's government and brought in Putin as his replacement in 2000.

The *siloviki* have taken over government. Their clients rule the regions, cities and towns and control the police and courts. They have steadily increased the staff and powers of the FSB, which today has 40 per cent more officers per citizen than the Soviet-era KGB. They have carried out a systematic assault on freedom of speech and information, intimidating independent newspapers and turning a blind eye to the contract killing of dozens of journalists, not to mention many more suspicious "accidents" over the past seven years.

The emerging political system is not yet a dictatorship, but nor is it democracy in anything but formal terms. Opposition parties can exist—but only within certain bounds. Elections are held—but their results are a foregone conclusion and the power-holders chosen in Kremlin corridors long before the polls open. There is no real political debate in the public media, and no broader culture of democracy to foster diversity of opinion. In many ways the problem is not the growing power of the Putin state (it could be argued that it is not as strong as it appears), but the chronic weakness of civil society. Sixteen years after the collapse of the Soviet regime, there are still no real social organisations, no mass-based political parties (except perhaps the Communists), no trade unions, no consumer or environmental groups, no professional bodies, and only a very small number of human rights associations, such as Memorial, to counteract the power of the state.

No Need to Pay

The second element of Putinism is the intimate connection between politics and business. Senior state officials control and own the public media, sit on the boards of state-owned corporations and enrich themselves from it, have lucrative

Russia's "Sovereign Democracy" Is Really Authoritarianism

The de facto appointment by Putin of Dmitri Medvedev to become Russia's next president has incited hopes that Russia's disconcerting foreign policy might begin to change. Yet even assuming that "President" Medvedev and not "Prime Minister" Putin will eventually formulate Russia's policies (something that is hard to imagine today), such expectations only underscore the very heavy and deeply entrenched legacy Medvedev, and the West, will have to tackle. . . .

[By 2005] the key postulates of the Russian political tradition were returning in force: the state guides society, not the other way around; all that is good for the state is automatically beneficial to society; and to strengthen the state means to strengthen the country. A state functionary, a bureaucrat (enlightened, intelligent, hardworking, and a model of probity, of course) is a far more effective and consistent agent of progress than a free press (so corrupt, sensationalist, and concerned with profits instead of the good of the country!); a voter (so naïve, uneducated, and fickle!); an independent judge (such a bribe-taker!); or, God forbid, a private entrepreneur (thinking of nothing else but his profit!).

In myriad articles, the Kremlin's paid and unpaid propagandists called this arrangement "sovereign democracy"—in essence, a still rather soft authoritarianism, increasingly with nationalistic and isolationist overtones. As an independent Russian analyst noted, such [analysis] "would have been labeled as fascist, chauvinistic, antidemocratic or anti-Western during Yeltsin's term. Now such texts have become mainstream."

Leon Aron, "Putin-3," American Enterprise Institute, Winter 2008.

connections with the oligarchs [Russia's super-rich who profited from the end of the Soviet era], and own large shares of the country's banks as well as its oil, gas and mining companies. At a lower level, in many Russian towns, politics and business are closely intertwined with the police and organised crime. Much of this goes well beyond corruption in the conventional meaning of the term (businessmen offering bribes to officials). In Putin's Russia the politician is usually a businessman, too, and perhaps an FSB official as well, so he doesn't need to pay a bribe. Political connections are the fastest way to become rich. The most successful oligarchs are shadowy figures in the presidential entourage. And all the country's senior politicians are multimillionaires, their money safely stashed abroad for them by Kremlin-favoured businessmen.

Thanks to the high price of oil and gas, Putin has overseen a strong upturn in the economy, which accounts for much of his popularity. The core of his constituency is the fast-growing middle class—the eight million Russians in 2000 and some 40 million [in 2007] who are doing well enough to own homes and cars and go abroad on holiday. But Putin is also popular among a broader section of the population that has been lifted out of poverty by the recovery of recent years. The hyperinflation and economic instability of the 1990s are a fading memory. The rouble [or ruble, Russian currency] is strong; reserves are huge; public sector salaries are paid on time and, like pensions, have increased under Putin; and the government is at last starting to invest in the country's creaking infrastructure, hospitals and schools.

Yet there are serious economic vulnerabilities, not least Russia's heavy dependence on the export of its natural resources and the weakness of its manufacturing, services and hi-tech industries. The most serious concern is an imminent demographic crisis, largely brought about by high death rates (in particular among men, the main vodka drinkers) and westward emigration from Russia by large sections of the young and talented. Since 1991, the population has fallen by ten million to 140 million. A UN [United Nations] report estimates that it could fall below 100 million by 2050. Already there are shortages of students at universities and of staff in the workplace in many areas.

Meanwhile the Muslim population, with its historically high birth rates, continues to grow, in part as immigrants from central Asia fill the gaps in the labour market. There are 25 million Muslims in Russia [as of November 2007] (demographers predict that they will be the majority within 50 years). Like the Jews in previous times, Russia's Muslims have become the focus of a rising wave of xenophobic Russian nationalism that is only partly satisfied by Putin's increasingly nationalist rhetoric. If it weren't for him, millions of Russians would vote for an ultra-nationalist—for instance, Vladimir Zhirinovsky, whose Liberal Democratic Party is expected to come second, or perhaps third behind the Communists, with roughly 10 per cent of the vote.

Humiliation

Nationalism is the third main element of Putinism, and perhaps the key to its success. Putin's nationalism is more complex than the reassertion of Russia's influence in the "near abroad" of former Soviet satellites (notably against the pro-western governments of Georgia and Ukraine) or the flexing of Russia's oil-pumped muscles on the international scene. At its heart is a long historical tradition of imperial rule and resentment of the west that has shaped the national consciousness.

The collapse of the Soviet Union was felt as a humiliation by most Russians. In a matter of a few months they lost everything—an empire, an ideology, an economic system, superpower status, national pride. They lost a national identity connected to the official myths of Soviet history: the liberating power of October 1917, victory in the Great Patriotic War, Soviet achievements in culture, science and technology. Within months of the Soviet collapse, the Russians had fallen into poverty and hunger and become dependent on relief from the west, which lectured them about democracy and human rights. Everything that happened in the 1990s—the hyperinflation, the loss of people's savings and security, the rampant corruption and criminality, the robber-oligarchs and the drunken president—was a source of national shame.

From the start, Putin understood the importance of historical rhetoric for his nationalist politics, particularly if it played to popular nostalgia for the Soviet Union. Polls in the year he came to power showed that three-quarters of the Russian population regretted the break-up of the USSR and wanted Russia to expand in size, incorporating "Russian" territories such as the Crimea and the Don Basin, which had been lost to Ukraine. Putin quickly built up his own historical mythology, combining Soviet myths (stripped of their Communist phraseology) with statist elements from the Russian empire before 1917. In this way his regime was connected to and sanctioned by a long historical continuum, a Russian tradition of strong state power, going back to the founder of the empire, Peter the Great, and Putin's native city, St Petersburg.

Integral to this is the idea, fostered by Putin, that Russia's traditions of authoritarian rule are morally the equal of democratic western traditions. Indeed, his supporters often say that Russians value a strong state, economic growth and security more than the liberal concepts of human rights or democracy, which have no roots in Russian history.

The rehabilitation of Stalin is the most disturbing element of Putin's historical rhetoric—and the most powerful, for it taps into a deep Russian yearning for a "strong leader." According to a survey in 2005, 42 per cent of the Russian people, and 60 per cent of those over 60 years of age, wanted the return of a "leader like Stalin." At a conference [in June 2007] Putin called on schoolteachers to portray the Stalin period in a more positive light. It was Stalin who made Russia great and his "mistakes" were no worse than the crimes of western states, he said. Textbooks dwelling on the Great Terror and the Gulag have been censored, historians attacked as anti-patriotic for highlighting Stalin's crimes.

All this comes as a huge relief to most Russians. Brought up on the Soviet myths, they felt ashamed, uncomfortable and resentful when, for a short time in the late 1980s and early 1990s, they were suddenly confronted by these awkward truths about their past. Now they needn't feel ashamed. With Putin's rewriting of Soviet history, they can feel good about their nation and themselves (as if, by way of a comparison, the post-war Germans had been told that the Holocaust had never taken place). Thanks to Putin, the Russians can move on and live their lives without asking awkward questions of themselves. It is how they lived in the Soviet Union.

Interviewing hundreds of survivors of Stalin's Terror [of the 1920s and 1930s when millions of alleged dissidents were imprisoned or killed] for my book *The Whisperers*, I encountered many legacies of the Stalin period that affect the way Russians think and act today. One of the most striking is a strong political conformity, a silent acceptance and lack of questioning of authority, which was born of fear in the Stalin period but then passed down the generations to become part of what one might call the post-Soviet personality. No doubt this conformism will play a part in the elections, and in the resolution of the power question in the months to come. If Putin chose to sweep away the constitution and declare himself a dictator, I doubt many Russians would protest.

| "*Russia is not in transition to or from anything.*"

Russia Is Not Becoming a Democracy *or* a Dictatorship

Stephen Kotkin

In the following viewpoint, Stephen Kotkin criticizes both "fashionable" media portrayals of Russia as a dangerous, increasingly authoritarian state and political scientists' teaching that Russia's growing, stable middle class means the country must be "on the road to law and democracy." Neither is true, he argues. Russian officials distrust, despise, and compete with one another, so there is no coherent "Kremlin Inc." controlling the state and the economy, and Russian society is more open than would be possible in a dictatorship. On the other hand, yes, roughly 25 percent of Russian society is solidly middle class, but the middle class wants stability and the preservation of its privileged access to good education, jobs, and property ownership; with half of the middle class employed by the state, Russians have too much at stake to push for democratic reforms. Russia "is what it is," Kotkin concludes, deeply apolitical but too committed to entrepreneurism, consumerism, and global networking to allow order to give way to dictatorship. Stephen Kotkin is a professor of history and the director of the Russian and Eurasian Studies program at Princeton University.

As you read, consider the following questions:

1. Kotkin objects to the portrayal of Russian politics as a KGB-dominated takeover of the government. What does he mean by describing Russia's political system as "personalistic" rather than "Kremlin Inc.?"
2. What social signs does Kotkin see as proof that "consolidation of dictatorship is not happening?"
3. In the author's view, even if there is growing state control of major industries such as Russia's gas monopoly, why can there be no return to a Soviet-style economy?

Russia is not a democracy, and it is not a dictatorship. Russia, like most countries of the world, has a ramshackle authoritarian system with some democratic trappings (some of which are meaningful). Russia is not in transition to or from anything. Russia is what it is.

Americans Have a Distorted View of Russian Politics

Here in the U.S., it seems much harder than it should be to get good information on and insight into Russia. For instance, while the U.S. is the world's number-one country in the number of immigrants it receives each year, Russia is second. Perhaps you knew that, but most likely you did not. "Immigrant nation" is not a way we in the U.S. talk about or understand today's Russia. Most of the immigrants to Russia come from former Soviet republics, like Ukraine, Armenia, or Tajikistan, though some also come from North Korea and China. Today more than 500,000 and perhaps up to 1 million Muslims are thought to live in Moscow! At the same time, more than a quarter million Russians live in London. These migratory patterns represent major shifts. They are tied to the huge story of the Russian economy, which is transregional and global, but which we often hear about through a political lens.

American reportage on Russia generally obsesses about the Kremlin and the [former] leader, Vladimir Putin. Putin dominates U.S. coverage of Russia far more than he dominates Russia. In the bargain, American media rarely quote Russians other than so-called talking heads distant from the high politics being obsessively covered. On policy matters there are almost no "senior Kremlin officials" quoted either by name or anonymously in American dispatches. Similarly, there are almost no heads of major businesses quoted. Court cases or tax cases do not cite law enforcement or state officials of any rank. Often not even agency spokesmen are quoted in the reporting. To be sure, some foreign reporters working in English on Russia do dig up facts, quote many sources close to events, and illuminate issues beyond the preoccupations of the U.S. government and bilateral relations. And there is hope that the circumstance of a semi-competitive or even simulated presidential election campaign will induce some Russian insiders to grant a degree of access to foreign media.

Access does not guarantee insight . . . but most reports on Russia continue to be virtually unsourced. If pressed about access challenges and a conspicuous lack of good sources, American reporters covering Russia might blame the Russians' penchant for secrecy. They would have a point. The hypersecretive Russian government is a marketing nightmare, guaranteeing the country as a whole a far worse reputation than it merits. In what follows—which is based upon firsthand observation and discussions with Russian officialdom—I present some broad-brush comments on three dimensions of understanding Russia: first, the phenomenon of so-called Kremlin Inc., the now fashionable notion that the Putin regime is like a big, single state corporation; second, the uncannily stable nature of today's Russian society, something we hear far less about; and third, Russia's new assertiveness, which has taken many people by surprise and which is sometimes perceived as a new threat.

Kremlin Inc.

"Kremlin Inc." is something that anyone can readily understand. It signifies that a KGB [former Soviet secret service] -dominated Putin group has taken over Russia and controls the country politically and economically. It's a wonderfully simple story, now perhaps the dominant view among U.S. commentators on Russia. But Kremlin Inc. is one of those pernicious half truths.

The Russian political system lacks functioning political parties or other institutionalized mechanisms of elite recruitment. Instead it has an extremely personalistic system. Russian leaders appoint to positions of authority those people they went to school with, those from their hometowns, those from the places where they used to work. Vladimir Putin came from St. Petersburg. Moreover, he was at the top levels in Moscow for only a short period before he became president. To assert operative control over central state institutions and state-owned corporations, he seeks to appoint people who are loyal to him (sometimes he gets lucky and gets both competence and loyalty, but often it's just loyalty). Such people naturally will come from his hometown and former places of work, which happened to be the Leningrad KGB and the St. Petersburg city government. . . .

The popular idea of a KGB takeover of the Russian political system makes a certain amount of sense. The Soviet KGB was a huge institution, with massive personnel, and so, inevitably, a lot of today's movers and shakers used to work there. But if Putin had worked in the defense ministry, the defense ministry would be "taking over" Russia. If he had worked in the gas industry, those who have made their careers in gas would be "taking over" Russia. It's wrong to assume that because Putin comes from the KGB, and because that's where his loyalists come from, the whole system is moving in the direction of a security regime by design. There is an element of that. Many of Putin's colleagues sometimes do share a certain mentality—distrust of the West—but even more significantly, they belong to competing factions.

And that's the key point. Whereas "Kremlin Inc." implies a team, united in a collective enterprise, most high Russian officials despise each other. They're rivals, in charge of competing fiefdoms with overlapping jurisdictions, and they're trying to destroy each other. Dictatorship 101 teaches that a dictator needs officials to distrust each other, so that they'll tattle to him about each other. The ruler will say "Don't worry, I'll take care of him, he won't bother you anymore." Sometimes the ruler will impose a temporary truce. Often, though, the ruler will instigate still more conflict, pitting already antagonistic interests against each other, so that they'll run to him for protection and become dependent on him.

Putin's regime falls far short of being a dictatorship—in the chaotic conditions of the dysfunctional Russian state and of Russia's relatively open society—but Putin's ruling strategy comes straight out of Dictatorship 101. To outsiders, the strategy looks like centralization of all power in a disciplined pyramid, but on the inside the strategy looks like making sure that the ruling "team," far from being united, is at each other's throats. Thus, "Kremlin Inc." is a political system of surface stability but turmoil underneath. Its members compete incessantly, and in Russian politics, offense is the best defense, so they proactively go after each other's property and people . . . before waiting for rivals to go after them. . . .

Russia's Mostly Stable Society

The part of Russia that is stable is the society. Russian society is enormously dynamic. According to professional studies by the Institute of Sociology of the Russian Academy of Sciences,

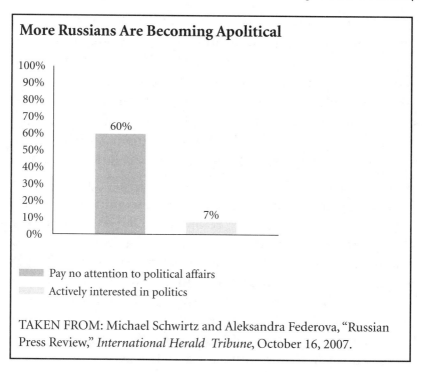

More Russians Are Becoming Apolitical

60%

7%

Pay no attention to political affairs

Actively interested in politics

TAKEN FROM: Michael Schwirtz and Aleksandra Federova, "Russian Press Review," *International Herald Tribune*, October 16, 2007.

something like 20–25 percent of Russian society qualifies as solidly middle class. Other studies—similarly measuring everything from level of education, foreign language knowledge, and travel abroad to income, lifestyle and, most important, property ownership—confirm this general picture. But the Russian middle class is something we hear too little about (unlike the middle class in, say, China or India). Instead, we hear about "oligarchs." The latter number in the dozens, while the middle class numbers in the dozens of millions.

Russia's middle class is not limited to the capital, although it's biggest there. You see it in all the regional centers that have a dynamic economy. You see it in western Siberia, in St. Petersburg and in the north around St. Petersburg, in pockets of central Russia, and in some border areas. That doesn't mean that the society has no poverty, that there aren't deep problems like an overall decline of the population at all ages— down to 142 million, and still shrinking, despite the immigration. But the country has a dynamic, stable society, and it owns property. We tend to assume that there cannot be property ownership without rule of law. But if that were true, Chinese society or Russian society would not exist. But they do exist. There is no rule of law. But there is widespread ownership of property. For all the deep social problems—from drug-resistant TB to persistent alcoholism—Russian society is simultaneously a source of dynamism and stability.

About half of the Russian middle class works for the state. They're bureaucrats and functionaries, law enforcement officials and tax collectors, inspectors and education overseers. They work in the KGB successor, the FSB, and in the big state-owned gas, oil, automobile, or defense companies. There's a gigantic private economy in Russia (Russia's economy is more private than China's). But even those who work in private companies usually work in very large corporations. A tiny fraction of the Russian middle class owns their own businesses, but by and large, Russia's middle class is not independent, small- or medium-sized business owners. Whereas in the United States and Western Europe, 70 percent of employment is in small and medium-sized businesses, Russia doesn't even approach 25 percent for such employment. Still, Russia has a stable, dynamic, growing, state and corporate middle class that has a tremendous stake in stability.

Putin deserves some credit for the current sense of and desire for continued social stability, and he gets such credit from middle class Russians and those aspiring to become so. Again, however, outsiders sometimes miss or misinterpret this point, because they are looking for democracy. American political science teaches that if a country gets a stable middle class, it is on the road to the rule of law and democracy. This is true except in all the cases where it's not true, which is most of the world. The Russian middle class knows Europe first-hand from traveling there, and for the most part its members identify with the values and institutions of democratic Europe. But the Russian middle class is smart, and it knows that if it gets political, it could lose its property and status. Individuals respond to incentives very well (economists are not totally wrong), and for the most part Russia's middle class is not ready to sacrifice its position to push for the rule of law and democracy; rather, it is interested in preserving its wealth, in privileged access for its children to educational institutions and to career paths. So there is no push in Russia for democracy either from the top or the middle, even though much of the middle identifies strongly with European values and institutions.

Consolidation of dictatorship is not happening either, and society is a factor in that as well. Russia has no ideology like communism to unify people around a strong dictator, the Russian state lacks the capacity to impose military-style discipline on itself, and Russia has a market economy that is extremely complex to subordinate in part because it's globalized. Even though there is a strong current in Russian society appreciative of order, few people mistake order for dictatorship. In fact, in conversations there is quite a lot of criticism in Russia of Putin and of the country's direction, especially from people who comprise the Russian state. Meanwhile, Russian society is transforming the country's socioeconomic landscape with its hard work, entrepreneurialism, consumption patterns and tastes, demand for education, foreign travel, and networking both domestically and globally. Russia's social transformation is a big story, hiding, once again, in plain view. It is enough to take in the commercial advertising throughout society and media, including on pro-Kremlin Russian television, to see that business interests are targeting something commentators are not: Russia's middle class.

Russia's New Assertiveness Is Not a Threat to the West

In the 1990s, NATO [the military alliance North Atlantic Treaty Organization] expansion should have been defended on the grounds that it would increase the strength and capacity of NATO. In the event, the expansion did no such thing. On the contrary, you could argue that expansion has weakened NATO because you have all these militaries that were brought into NATO that don't meet NATO specifications and have little to contribute. One key argument against NATO expansion in the 1990s was "It will anger the Russians and make them really mad at us, and they'll do some bad things. So placate the Russians and don't expand NATO." . . . Today when people say "Now Russia is flexing its muscles, it's again trying to be involved in all regions of the world, NATO shouldn't have expanded," my response is that had there been no NATO expansion, we would likely still have what we see now in Russia: a revived, assertive, resentful power.

This revived, assertive, resentful Russia is nothing to fear. Russia has state interests that are different from U.S. interests (or Japanese interests or Chinese interests). Russians are more assertive in pressing their perceived state interests, but are they effective in doing so? Have they persuaded Europe that they're a partner in energy security by cutting off the gas to Ukraine [which Russia did in 2006], or are they using their energy muscle in a way that could be compared to stepping on a rake? When you step on a rake, you smack yourself in the forehead. That's Russian foreign policy. They smack themselves in the forehead.

Energy supply looks like a point of tremendous leverage for Russia, except energy's a market, which entails a kind of codependency relationship. Russian suppliers have to find customers, and those customers have to not find alternatives, either in somebody else's hydrocarbons or alternative forms. Silly talk about a "gas OPEC" [Arab-led Organization of Petroleum Exporting Countries]—Russia has refused to join the regular OPEC—is a diversion, usually failing to enumerate the various ways that a gas OPEC is an impossibility, and the ways that the idea, not dismissed by Putin, goes down well in Tehran. An even more fundamental point often missed is that

Russia cannot be your old Soviet economy anymore. Russia can form as many big state companies as it wants, but if Russia's state-owned companies fail to perform in market conditions, the market will eventually punish them. The old joke about the State Planning Commission, so-called Gosplan, was that if you put them in charge of the Sahara, there would be a shortage of sand. Well, Gazprom, the gas monopoly, is in charge of the gas in a country that has around 33 percent of world gas reserves, and Russia may be running out of gas. The problem with a market economy is that you actually have to run a company as a business, and if you do not, you will pay the price.

When the Russian government gets assertive, mostly rhetorically, there's little cause to worry, or even to react. Sure, other countries need to try to understand what Russian state interests are, so that there can be productive state-to-state relations based on mutual interests. But this is no different from relations with China, India, or any major country that seeks a place in an international system that these major powers did not create but that cannot function without their inclusion. A new cold war does not happen simply because Russia is suddenly semi-assertive again. Russia's military is a shambles. Russia's territory is much reduced, it controls no empire or satellites, and it barely has a sphere of influence. It lacks meaningful alliances. Its current political-economic model does not appeal to developing countries. True, Russia's GDP [gross domestic product] has been growing at a rapid pace for eight years, but this is a good thing. In the belated recognition that Russia is a petrostate, the degree of diversification of Russia's economy (biotech, software, aerospace, military hardware, food processing) is often missed. That, not posturing, will be the basis of Russian power, or lack thereof.

The overall picture in Russia, therefore, is, first, a false stability in the regime but actual instability. . . . Russia has a dynamic middle-class society that is stable, and mostly apolitical.

The middle class in Russia understands that for now being apolitical is a winning strategy, and so it is deeply apolitical, to the disappointment of human rights and democracy activists. Third, the world will have to get used to the newly assertive Russia. Russia is not what it was in the 1990s, when it was free-falling, in an ongoing post-Soviet collapse, but rather it is a strategic power in a very important location, with its own state interests, interests that are going to conflict with others' interests sometimes. Still, there is no need to be alarmed. The problem with viewing Russia as a major threat is that the threat is mostly to itself, not to the outside world.

> *"[The presidential oath's] very first lines pledge respect and protection of human rights and freedoms. . . . They determine the sense and the substance of all state policy."*

The Kremlin Respects Russians' Civil Rights

Dmitry Medvedev

The following viewpoint is the text of Dmitry Medvedev's inaugural address, in which he commits himself to the protection of Russians' civil rights and the development of an impartial, effective legal system. Medvedev was sworn in as president of Russia on May 7, 2008, succeeding Vladimir Putin.

As you read, consider the following questions:

1. What does Medvedev hope to achieve by improving Russians' living standards?

2. What benefits of a "mature and effective legal system," both domestic and international, does Medvedev cite?

3. According to the president, Russia's future depends on the cooperation of which groups?

Dmitry Medvedev, "Speech at Inauguration Ceremony as President of Russia," Official Web Portal of the President of Russia, www.kremlin.ru, May 7, 2008.

Citizens of Russia, friends!

I have just sworn the presidential oath, the oath taken before the people of Russia, and its very first lines pledge respect and protection of human rights and freedoms. It is them that our society declares the greatest value, and they determine the sense and the substance of all state policy.

It is for this reason that I consider it my greatest duty to continue to develop civil and economic freedom and to create the broadest new opportunities for our people to realise their full potential as free citizens responsible for their personal success and for the prosperity of our entire country.

It is these citizens who create the nation's greatest worth and who are the source of strength of a state that today possesses the resources it needs and a clear understanding of our national interests.

I want to assure all of our citizens today that I will spare no effort in my work as President and as someone for whom Russia is my home and my native soil.

Over these last eight years we have laid a solid foundation for long-term construction, for free and stable development in the decades to come. We must make full use of this unique opportunity to turn Russia into one of the world's best countries; best in providing its people with comfort, confidence and security in their lives. This is our strategy and this is the goal that will guide us in the years ahead.

I am fully aware of just how much still needs to be done to make our state truly just and caring towards its citizens and provide the highest possible living standards so that more and more people can swell the ranks of the middle class and gain access to good education and healthcare services.

We are committed to innovation in all areas of life, to developing cutting-edge production, modernising our industry and agriculture, creating big incentives for private investment

The Russian Constitution Guarantees Citizens' Rights and Freedoms

Article 17

1. In the Russian Federation human and civil rights and freedoms shall be recognized and guaranteed according to the universally recognized principles and norms of international law and this Constitution.

2. Basic human rights and freedoms shall be inalienable and shall be enjoyed by everyone from birth.

3. The exercise of human and civil rights and freedoms must not violate the rights and freedoms of other people. . . .

Article 19

1. All persons shall be equal before the law and the court.

2. The State guarantees the equality of human and civil rights and freedoms regardless of sex, race, nationality, language, origin, material and official status, place of residence, attitude to religion, convictions, membership of public associations, or of other circumstances. All forms of limitations of human rights on social, racial, national, language or religious grounds shall be prohibited.

3. Men and women shall enjoy equal rights and freedoms and equal opportunities to exercise them. . . .

"Rights and Freedoms of Man and Citizen,"
Articles 17–64, The Constitution of Russia,
Official Web Portal of the President of Russia. *www.kremlin.ru.*

and generally making every effort to help Russia firmly establish itself as a leader in technological and intellectual development.

The Fundamental Role of the Law

I place particular importance on the fundamental role of the law, which is the cornerstone of our state and our civil society. We must ensure true respect for the law and overcome the legal nihilism that is such a serious hindrance to modern development.

A mature and effective legal system is an essential condition for economic and social development, supporting entrepreneurship and fighting corruption. But it is no less important for increasing Russia's influence in the international community, making our country more open to the world and facilitating dialogue as equals with other peoples.

Finally, true supremacy of the law is only possible if people feel safe in their lives. I will do everything I can to ensure that the safety of our citizens is not just enshrined in the law but genuinely guaranteed by the state.

These tasks I have named call for day-to-day cooperation with all the responsible political forces in our society, with all the institutions of civil society and with the parties and the country's regions.

I hope that cooperation between our country's different religious faiths and social and ethnic groups will continue to strengthen peace and harmony in our common home. Our country's present and future depend on it.

Dear friends! You can understand what profound emotion I feel at this time. I am very conscious of the weight of responsibility that will fall upon my shoulders, and I count on our work together.

I give my sincere thanks to President Vladimir Vladimirovich Putin for the unfailing personal support I have always received from him. I am sure that this will not change

Life and the march of history place us before fundamentally new and even more complex tasks. But I am sure that our country and its hardworking and talented people are entirely up to these tasks.

My duty now is to serve our people every day and every hour, and do everything possible to give them a better life, success and confidence in the future, in the name of the continued rise and prosperity of our beloved homeland, our great Russia.

> "*[Putin] issues a law allowing the Russians to kill opponents abroad. So they kill opponents abroad.*"

The Kremlin Assassinates Its Critics

Michael Specter

In the following viewpoint, American journalist Michael Specter describes the recent poisoning and murders of Russian dissident journalists and officials, including reporter Anna Politkovskaya, politician Viktor Yushchenko, and former KGB agent Alexander Litvenenko, under suspicious circumstances. According to Specter, conspiracy theories abound, many of which point to the Russian secret service presumably acting on orders of former president Vladimir Putin, who is accused of condoning violence to silence his critics. Though Putin and various Kremlin officials deny any involvement, Specter's contacts say Putin's history as a KGB officer, his track record of curtailing press freedoms, and his support of a 2006 law that permits the assassination of "enemies of the Russian regime" have tarnished his reputation and raised suspicions in the West. Michael Specter has been a staff writer

Michael Specter, "Kremlin, Inc.," *New Yorker,* January 29, 2007, pp. 51–53, 57, 62.

for The New Yorker *since 1998. He was formerly co-chief of the* New York Times *Moscow bureau, where he covered the war in Chechnya and Russian presidential politics.*

As you read, consider the following questions:

1. What did Anna Politkovskaya do to become the target of state-sponsored violence, according to the author's description?

2. According to political science professor Evgenia Albats, quoted by Specter, what happened to the old KGB after the fall of the Soviet Union?

3. Why does the identification of the poison that killed Alexander Litvenenko as polonium 210 suggest Kremlin involvement, according to Specter?

[In October 2006, Russian journalist Anna Politkovskaya] was a special correspondent for the small liberal newspaper *Novaya Gazeta*, and, like most of her work, [her current] piece focussed on the terror that pervades the southern republic of Chechnya. This time, she had been trying to document repeated acts of torture carried out by squads loyal to the pro-Russian Prime Minister, Ramzan Kadyrov. In the past seven years, Politkovskaya had written dozens of accounts of life during wartime; many had been collected in her book *A Small Corner of Hell: Dispatches from Chechnya*. Politkovskaya was far more likely to spend time in a hospital than on a battlefield, and her writing bore frequent witness to robbery, rape, and the unbridled cruelty of life in a place that few other Russians—and almost no other reporters—cared to think about. . . .

In the West, Politkovskaya's honesty brought her a measure of fame and a string of awards, bestowed at ceremonies in hotel ballrooms from New York to Stockholm. At home, she had none of that. Her excoriations of Russia's President, Vladimir Putin, insured isolation, harassment, and, many predicted, death. "I am a pariah," she wrote in an essay [in 2005]. "That is the result of my journalism through the years of the Second Chechen War, and of publishing books abroad about life in Russia." Despite the fact that Politkovskaya was articulate, attractive, and accomplished, she was barred from appearing on television, which is the only way the vast majority of Russians get news. To the degree that a living woman could be airbrushed out of post-Soviet history, she had been. "People call the newspaper and send letters with one and the same question: 'Why are you writing about this? Why are you scaring us?'" she wrote. "'Why do we need to know this?'" She provided an answer as much for herself as for any reader: "I'm sure this has to be done, for one simple reason: as contemporaries of this war, we will be held responsible for it. The classic Soviet excuse of not being there and not taking part in anything personally won't work. So I want you to know the truth. Then you'll be free of cynicism."

[On October 7, 2006], Politkovskaya drove to a supermarket near her mother's apartment, on the Frunzenskaya Embankment. Her daughter had planned to meet her there but was delayed. Nonetheless, as a surveillance camera at the store later showed, Politkovskaya was not alone. A young woman and a tall, slender man whose face was obscured by a baseball cap lurked in the aisles as she shopped. When Politkovskaya finished, she drove home in her silver Vaz 2110 and parked a few feet from the entrance to her building. She carried two bags of groceries up to her apartment, on the seventh floor, in the building's tiny elevator and dropped them at the door. Then she went down to fetch the rest of her parcels. When the elevator opened on the ground floor, her killer was waiting. He shot her four times—the first two bullets piercing her heart and lungs, the third shattering her shoulder, with a force that drove Politkovskaya back into the elevator. He then administered what is referred to in Moscow, where contract killings have become routine, as the *kontrolnyi vystrel*—control

A History of State-Sponsored Assassination

In a report released [in November 2006] the United Nations' Committee Against Torture accused Russia of torturing detainees, charged that people continued to disappear in [Russian republic] Chechnya and urged Russia to address numerous reports of hazing in the military and the harassment and killing of rights activists. . . .

Russia has [many times] been accused of assassination attempts beyond its borders. . . .

In 2004, a car bomb killed Zelimkhan Yandarbiyev, former Chechen separatist president, in Qatar. Two Russian FSB agents were arrested and convicted in Qatar but later were released after intense diplomatic pressure from Russia. Later that year, pro-Western Ukrainian presidential candidate Viktor Yushchenko was hospitalized with dioxin poisoning, which disfigured his face and nearly killed him. Many fingers pointed at the Kremlin, which had strongly supported Yushchenko's opponent, Viktor Yanukovych (who is now Ukraine's prime minister).

Anna Badkhen, "Russia—The Usual Suspected Assassin,"
SFGate.com, November 29, 2006.

shot. He fired a bullet into her head from inches away. Then he dropped his weapon, a plastic 9-mm. Makarov pistol whose serial number had been filed away, and slipped into the darkening afternoon.

Thirteen Murdered Journalists

The murder of Anna Politkovskaya was at once unbelievable and utterly expected. She had been hunted and attacked before. In 2001, she fled to Vienna after receiving e-mailed threats claiming that a special-services police officer whom she had accused of committing atrocities against civilians (and who was eventually convicted of the crimes) was bent on revenge. While she was abroad, a woman who looked very much like her was shot and killed in front of Politkovskaya's Moscow apartment building. Police investigators believe the bullet was meant for Politkovskaya. In 2004, she became violently ill after drinking tea on a flight to Beslan, in North Ossetia, where, at the request of Chechen leaders, she was to negotiate with terrorists who had seized a school and taken more than eleven hundred hostages, most of them children. The Russian Army, which had bungled its response to the siege, did not want her there. Upon landing in Rostov, she was rushed to the hospital; the next day, she was flown by private jet to Moscow for treatment. By the time she arrived, her blood-test results and other medical records had somehow disappeared. She survived, only to be called a "midwife to terror." The threats became continuous: calls in the middle of the night, letters, e-mails, all ominous, all promising the worst. "Anna knew the risks only too well," her sister told me. Politkovskaya was born in New York while her father was serving at the United Nations, in 1958; not long ago, her family persuaded her to obtain an American passport. "But that was as far as she would go," [her sister Elena] Kudimova said. "We all begged her to stop. We begged. My parents. Her editors. Her children. But she always answered the same way: 'How could I live with myself if I didn't write the truth?'"

Since 1999, when Vladimir Putin, a career K.G.B. [the former Soviet Union's secret service] officer, was, in effect, anointed as President by Boris Yeltsin, thirteen journalists have been murdered in Russia. Nearly all the deaths took place in strange circumstances, and none of them have been successfully investigated or prosecuted. In July, 2003, the investigative reporter Yuri Shchekochikhin, a well-known colleague of Politkovskaya's at *Novaya Gazeta*, died of what doctors described as an "allergic reaction." Shchekochikhin, who became famous in the Gorbachev era with his reports on the rise of a new mafia, had been investigating allegations of tax evasion against people with links to the F.S.B., the post-Soviet K.G.B. Nobody ever explained what Shchekochikhin was allergic to, and his family is convinced that he was poisoned. On July 9, 2004, Paul Klebnikov, the founding editor of the Russian edition of *Forbes*—who had made powerful enemies by investigating corruption among Russian business tycoons—was shot dead as he left his Moscow office.

Murdered Officials and Dissidents

The attacks have not been limited to journalists. In September of 2004, Viktor Yushchenko, a candidate for President of Ukraine who helped lead the Orange Revolution [a series of protests following what many felt was a riggged election in 2004], and who was vigorously opposed by Putin, barely survived a poisoning. Doctors determined that he had been given the deadly chemical dioxin, which left his face disfigured and his health severely impaired. Since then, two members of the Duma, the Russian parliament, have been assassinated, and in September 2006 Andrei Kozlov, the deputy chief of Russia's central bank, was shot outside a Moscow stadium following a company soccer match. Kozlov had initiated a highly visible effort to rid the country of banks that were little more than fronts for organized crime. And [in late 2006] in an execution that could have been planned by Al Capone, Movladi Baisarov, a former Chechen special-forces officer who had come to be seen by [the pro-Russian Prime Minister Ramzan] Kadyrov as a rival, was gunned down on Leninsky Prospekt, one of Moscow's busiest thoroughfares. A series of control shots were administered in front of scores of witnesses, including high-ranking members of the police force. No arrests have been made.

Four weeks after Politkovskaya died, Alexander Litvinenko, a little-known former K.G.B. agent who had been imprisoned by Putin and had then defected to England, fell gravely ill in London. Like many others, including Politkovskaya, Litvinenko had accused the Russian President of creating a pretext for the Second Chechen War in 1999 by blowing up buildings in Moscow and then blaming Chechen separatists for the attacks. Putin's decisive response to those acts of terrorism propelled him toward immense and lasting popularity. He was outraged by Litvinenko's accusation and equally angered that Litvinenko had fallen into the orbit of Boris Berezovsky, one of his most despised enemies. Berezovsky, a shady billionaire oligarch, wielded huge power in the Yeltsin years, helped bring Putin to Yeltsin's attention, and even played a major role in persuading him to assume the Presidency. Once Putin took power, though, Berezovsky found himself shut off from the Kremlin; he accused Putin of turning his back on Yeltsin's reforms, and was driven from the country. Litvinenko subsequently charged that his F.S.B. superiors had ordered him to kill Berezovsky. On his deathbed, he lashed out at Putin, saying, "You have shown yourself to be as barbaric and ruthless as your most hostile critics have claimed."

The manner of Litvinenko's poisoning was obscure almost until the moment he died. At first, doctors thought that he had an unusual bacterial infection; then they said that his symptoms pointed toward rat poison. When his immune system started to fail, they thought it more likely that the poison was a radioactive form of thallium, which had been used by the K.G.B. nearly fifty years earlier in a failed attempt to assassinate Nikolai Khokhlov, an agent who had refused to comply with an order to kill a prominent Russian dissident. Finally, just hours before Litvinenko died, the doctors provided a definitive and even more improbable diagnosis: he had been poisoned with polonium 210, a rare radioactive isotope; a millionth of a gram is enough to destroy a person's bodily organs. Litvinenko's murder was the first known case of nuclear terrorism perpetrated against an individual.

Suspicion Falls on the Kremlin

In Moscow, a city given to conspiracy theories, people could speak of little else: Putin had acted to silence a vocal traitor; no, Putin's enemies did it, to destroy the image of the Kremlin and gain leverage in the 2008 Presidential campaign; Putin's allies did it, so that they could use the affair as a convenient excuse to ignore the constitution and secure him a third term; the "Jews" did it, because Litvinenko had converted to Islam; Muslim extremists did it, because Litvinenko had reneged on a promise to supply parts for a dirty bomb; Berezovsky did it, to embarrass Putin. The Kremlin even suggested that Leonid Nevzlin, a wealthy oil executive who fled Russia and lives in Israel, might have been involved. There was no proof for any of these assertions. [In July 2006] however, the Duma passed a law, introduced by the Kremlin, to permit the assassination of "enemies of the Russian regime" abroad. For people like Boris Berezovsky, whose hatred for Putin has become an obsession, the new law explained everything.

"This guy is a K.G.B. guy," Berezovsky told me one afternoon over tea at a London hotel. "This guy issues a law allowing the Russians to kill opponents abroad. *So they kill opponents abroad.*" His voice rose, and he shrugged, and then he glanced at me as if to say, How could one draw any other conclusion? "This is absolutely logical. Why did they issue this law? For what? Because this is Russia and nobody agrees to kill without the signature of somebody more important who gave the order." The Kremlin has denied any involvement in Litvinenko's death. Whatever the truth, the manner in which he died has tarnished Putin's reputation in the West. And so has the execution of a journalist who had been accused of nothing more than doing her job. . . .

Russia's Secret Services Are in "Full Power"

Politkovskaya, like many others, attributed the precipitate decline of press freedoms to Putin's background and his reflexes. In her book *Putin's Russia: Life in a Failing Democracy* (2004), she wrote that he is "a product of the country's murkiest intelligence service," and "has failed to transcend his origins and stop behaving like a K.G.B. officer." Putin has indeed presided over a remarkable resurgence in the power of the secret services, and many current Russian leaders are products of the K.G.B. and its successors.

"Reform of the K.G.B. never really happened," Evgenia Albats, a professor of political science at Moscow's Higher School of Economics, said [in 2006] after the deaths of Politkovskaya and Litvinenko. Albats has written more incisively about the K.G.B. than any other Russian journalist. "The organization was broken into several agencies in the early nineteen-nineties, but the reforms were abandoned, especially after Putin became President," she went on. "The K.G.B.'s capacity to be a political organization is back. And, unlike in the Soviet era, the secret services are now in full power." . . .

Polonium 210 is not easy to acquire—at least, not the amount necessary to kill a man. Nearly all of it is produced in Russia. Even though the amount necessary to kill Litvinenko was minuscule, it would almost certainly have required a sophisticated organization to procure, transport, prepare, measure, and administer it. Most people in London, and many in Moscow as well, believe that that organization was the F.S.B. Its members reserve special hatred for those who turn on it, and Litvinenko was a very high-profile traitor. He had accused the Russian President—a member of their secret fraternity—of killing his own citizens to start a war, and he had joined with the forces of Berezovsky. The F.S.B. had the motive, the skills, and the money.

"You know, for the first time in my life I really watched how the mass media in a free country works," Berezovsky told me when we met in London. "When Litvinenko died, there were a thousand theories: He killed himself, I killed him. Al Qaeda. Jews. Putin. Everybody. But the free press has competition, and step by step it started to get rid of the stupid versions and go to the mainstream: Kremlin. Kremlin. Kremlin. I was impressed. These are people who don't even understand about Russia, and yet, step by step, they got there. And in Russia it's the opposite. The press presents an artificial story, and if you open a Russian newspaper you just have to laugh."

Initially, Berezovsky did not believe that the F.S.B. was involved in the murder—it was too obvious and sensational, certain to bring Russia and Putin unwanted publicity. Then he learned that the job had been botched. "I think that the people who were planning to eliminate [him] were sure that nobody would be able to trace anything," he said. "They screwed up. They underestimated the British doctors, and they also overestimated their own talents, which is common. Nobody expected so many traces left. It was clearly a sloppy job. So what happened is that they outsmarted themselves. The polonium was discovered three hours before [Litvinenko] died. Three hours. If he had died in the first week or the second week, nobody would ever have known a thing."

"Repressive laws and practices presented by authorities as the price that the public has to pay in the war on terror can bring only limited short-term gains . . . while producing a lasting detrimental effect on freedoms and civil liberties in Russia."

Russia Is Fighting Terrorism Undemocratically and Unsuccessfully

Nabi Abdullaev and Simon Saradzhyan

In the following viewpoint, the authors argue that the Kremlin's heavy-handed approach to the war on terror amounts to unconstitutional restrictions on freedoms of speech, association, movement, due process, and the press. This in turn acts as an invitation to Russian law enforcement and intelligence agencies to use excessive violence, squash legitimate dissent, and harass whistleblowers, and is a catalyst for the proliferation of terrorist networks among resentful extremists who, as a consequence, are more likely to be seen as freedom fighters against government re-

Nabi Abdullaev and Simon Saradzhyan, "The Trade-Offs Between Security and Civil Liberties in Russia's War on Terror: The Regional Dimension," *Demokratizatsiya,* vol. 14, Summer 2006, pp. 361–406. Copyright © 2006 by Helen Dwight Reid Educational Foundation. Reproduced with permission of the Terrorism, Transnational Crime and Corruption Center (TRACC).

*pression. Nabi Abdullaev and Simon Saradzhyan are Moscow-based security and Russian political analysts and contributors to the Swiss research institute International Relations and Security Network (ISN). Abdullaev, a native of Dagestan in the North Causasus, is a former Harvard University fellow, and the Mos-*cow Times' *leading writer on terrorism, extremism, and human rights.*

As you read, consider the following questions:

1. What provisions of the 2002 law against extremism (strengthened in 2006) do the authors cite as inviting overly broad violations of citizens' rights?

2. What statistics do Abdullaev and Saradzhyan cite to show that the Russian people are prepared to accept even more curtailment of their liberties?

3. In the authors' view, how can Russia fight terrorism without suppressing individual and collective freedoms?

Almost every major terrorist attack in Russia has sparked a debate among policymakers on how to stem the tide of terrorism. With [Vladimir] Putin's ascent to the presidency [in 2000], and the subsequent consolidation of the executive and legislative branches, this debate ended with calls for new laws boosting law enforcement's powers at the expense of individual liberties. Even the 2004 Beslan massacre [in which Chechen separatists occupied a school and over 330 hostages died] failed to convince federal authorities that terrorism cannot be reined in by mechanical increases in law-enforcement agencies' budgets and powers.

Admittedly, the Kremlin's post-Beslan policy was more multifaceted than previous responses to terrorist attacks. The authorities, for example, attempted to identify the root causes of this horrific act rather than dismiss it as an act of fanaticism. Overall, however, the government continued to rely on a heavy-handed approach, calling for the further centralization

149

of the Kremlin's power at the expense of regional administrations and strengthening its coercive forces (i.e., law-enforcement agencies) at the expense of individual liberties. Instead of being subjected to fundamental, systemic reform, the law-enforcement agencies are routinely given more power and money in the hope that their abilities to prevent terrorist attacks will improve.

Restrictions on Media Are Excessive

Among other measures, the Putin administration has scrapped the popular election of governors . . . and restricted media coverage of terrorist acts. While submitting these and other measures in the form of bills to the Parliament, President Putin and members of his government also put pressure on regional elites and the mass media to toe the Kremlin's line on what it describes as a "war against international terrorism." For instance, Putin accused one of Russia's national channels of making money on blood after NTV broadcast from the Dubrovka theater [hostage crisis in 2002] in Moscow seconds before a commando raid.

Following that terrorist act, the Russian Parliament passed a raft of amendments to federal laws on media and on terrorism that would have imposed severe restrictions on coverage of terrorist acts. Putin vetoed the bill in November 2002, but he made it clear that he was upset with the coverage.

Russia's leading broadcast media responded in April 2003 by adopting a convention that set strict rules for covering terrorist acts and antiterrorist operations. The coverage of the Beslan massacre differed from the Dubrovka attack. NTV was the only national channel that provided almost nonstop coverage of the tragedy in Beslan, where more than 1,200 hostages were held by a group of terrorists. One of NTVs anchors, Ruslan Gusarov, humbly asked a security officer in a live interview if the official thought NTV had committed any violations in its coverage.

Overly Broad Definitions of Terrorism and Extremism

The law on countering extremism has become a landmark in terms of expanding law enforcement's powers in the day-to-day war on terror. The law, passed in July 2002, has such a broad definition of terrorism that law-enforcement agencies can apply it to a broad spectrum of political and religious organizations and individuals. The law bans the dissemination of information that "substantiates or justifies ethnic or racial superiority," regardless of whether this information poses a threat. This provision allows prosecutors to classify many religious texts as extremist material. This provision obstructs an individual's right to collect and disseminate information.

The law also defines any activity that "undermine[s] the security of the Russian Federation" as extremist. Law-enforcement agencies have used this vaguely worded definition to harass environmental whistle-blowers who have exposed cases of toxic and radioactive waste dumped by the Russian military. This provision can also be used to prosecute anyone who harshly criticizes the conduct of individual officials or the authorities and, thus, it obstructs the freedom of speech.

Another provision of this law expands the range of groups and individuals who can be prosecuted for assisting in extremist activities. This assistance can be defined very broadly, covering, for instance, those whose only relationship with a terrorist is as a landlord, or even someone who provides funds or office equipment without knowing that they would be used for extremist activities. Such people can be identified as extremists and found liable under this law.

The law also allows the authorities to liquidate any organization suspected of extremist activities, violating citizens' right to association. The Prosecutor General's Office or Justice Ministry can find an organization in violation of the law and issue it a warning. If the warning remains unheeded, either agency can issue a second warning and, then, go to court and ask for the organization to be shut down. The law also allows prosecutors to suspend the organization's activities without a warrant, but the organization can appeal such a decision.

The procedure for closing a media outlet is very similar to shutting down an organization suspected of extremism. A warning may be issued in response to a publication or broadcast that supervisory authorities consider to be "substantiating or justifying a need for extremist activities." There have been cases when law-enforcement and security agencies have gone beyond this wide range of powers granted to them by the antiextremism law and other legislation.

Expanding Law Enforcement Powers Leads to Police Brutality

Two other key bills passed in 2000–2004 by the Parliament and signed into law by President Putin as part of the legal response to the escalation of terrorism include numerous amendments to the Criminal Code and the Criminal Procedures Code and give longer sentences to convicted terrorists. These amendments allow police to keep terrorism suspects in custody for up to thirty days without charging them. In comparison, those suspected of other crimes can be detained for up to three days without being charged. This measure clearly violates the freedom of movement and an individual's right to impartial justice, allowing investigators to put more pressure on a suspect in custody and giving them time to produce evidence in cases where they lack it. In 2004 the State Duma [parliament] passed an initial draft of a new and more repressive Law on Countering Terrorism that replaced the existing 1998 law. The bill would allow the FSB [federal security service] to declare a state of emergency in an area threatened by terrorist danger for up to sixty days, based on information—even if unverified—about preparations for a terrorist attack.

Law-enforcement officials in the North Caucasus [region which includes Chechnya] have relied on existing laws in their efforts to fight terrorism. They also abused their powers by cracking down on dissent that is unrelated to terrorism, as demonstrated in the Dagestan section. In Chechnya, law-enforcement agencies have conducted extrajudicial executions during the shift from large-scale operations to seek-and-destroy patrols. . . .

[In 2004–2004] Russian authorities gave the law-enforcement and defense agencies tacit approval to assassinate suspected terrorist leaders both in Russia and abroad. While the FSB did not hesitate to assume responsibility for killing Jordanian-born warlord Khattab in Chechnya, no Russian agency would admit to killing the vice president of Chechnya's self-proclaimed separatist government, Zelimkhan Yandar-biyev, in Qatar in February 2004. While refusing to assume responsibility, Russian authorities demanded, and succeeded in obtaining, the transfer of two Russian agents convicted of the assassination back to Russia under a Qatari court order.

Overall, despite some targeted operations, law enforcement's response to the escalation of terrorist attacks and conventional guerrilla operations remains excessive and indiscriminate.

There should be no doubt that the federal authorities are aware of the scale of abuses suffered by residents of the North Caucasus at the hands of local authorities and law enforcement, especially in Chechnya, Dagestan, and Ingushetia.

However, the Kremlin ignores these abuses in a tacit trade-off, whereby Moscow provides weapons, funds, and a legitimacy that comes with being a government employee while local authorities demonstrate loyalty by brutally suppressing political dissent. However, this arrangement is failing. The dynamics of terrorist networks in these three regions and several neighboring areas in the North Caucasus clearly demonstrated in the researched period that they were on the brink of be-

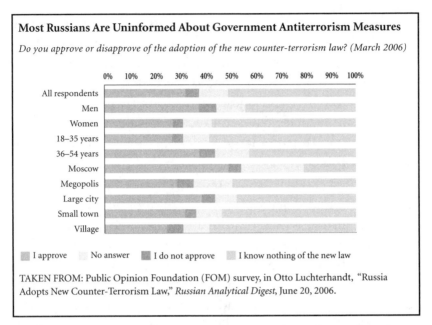

Most Russians Are Uninformed About Government Antiterrorism Measures

Do you approve or disapprove of the adoption of the new counter-terrorism law? (March 2006)

Legend: I approve   No answer   I do not approve   I know nothing of the new law

TAKEN FROM: Public Opinion Foundation (FOM) survey, in Otto Luchterhandt, "Russia Adopts New Counter-Terrorism Law," *Russian Analytical Digest*, June 20, 2006.

coming failed republics. Local leaders are as abusive and corrupt as leaders in the 1990s, but they are also becoming increasingly impotent. They cannot curb the escalation of terrorism.

Popular Indifference to Lost Liberties

Paradoxically, federal and local authorities, while broadening their powers to react and, to a far lesser extent, interdict terrorist groups, do relatively little to deter terrorism, especially through economic and financial development. Companies and organizations whose associates are found guilty or charged with terrorism can expect investigations into their finances. As of 2005, Russian law prohibited the indiscriminate confiscation of property of convicted terrorists, which could be a much more effective tool for discouraging potential sponsors or accomplices than fines or liquidation of companies. One reason such a repressive measure had not been introduced as of 2005 is that the Russian public largely opposes confiscation, fearing extension of this measure to other crimes. Yet the

Prosecutor General's Office and other law-enforcement agencies repeatedly called for the reintroduction of confiscation in the researched period.

In fact, the collateral damage inflicted on liberties and freedoms in this war on terror raises questions about the potential for further damage. One question is whether the authorities are striving to tighten their grip on the Russian public, which is, on one hand, becoming less sensitive to the growing death toll in the ongoing war on terror in the North Caucasus, but, on the other, is prepared for a further curtailment of liberties if it stems terrorism. A nationwide poll conducted by the independent Levada Center after the Beslan tragedy revealed that 58 percent believe that the moratorium on capital punishment should be lifted. Another 26 percent responded that terrorist's relatives should be punished. Thirty-three percent would ban Chechens from either traveling or living in Russian cities. A nationwide poll on terrorism conducted by the state-controlled All-Russia Public Opinion Research Center (VTsIOM) revealed an even greater preparedness to sacrifice freedoms for security. The September 2004 poll showed that 84 percent would favor the execution of terrorists even though a moratorium on capital punishment is a prerequisite for Russia's membership in the Council of Europe (CoE). Another 44 percent said they would support media censorship to support the war on terror. Thirty-five percent would support tougher ID checks, phone tapping, and body searches.

Thirty-three percent indicated they would support the suspension of opposition political organizations to fight terrorism. Such a formidable percentage demonstrates how incumbent officials can use the war on terror when running for reelection.

The repressive laws and practices presented by authorities as the price that the public has to pay in the war on terror can bring only limited short-term gains in this war, while producing a lasting detrimental effect on freedoms and civil liberties in Russia. Moreover, given the fact that Russia is in a state of transition, the intended and unintended effects of the authorities' antiterror policies could determine the course of Russia's political development. . . .

Heavy-Handed Suppression Will Incite, Not Defeat, Terrorism

The policy of suppressing liberties to enhance security is flawed.

The absence of stringent official and public oversight allows law-enforcement agencies to use excessive violence, which not only failed during the researched period to diminish the existing terrorist threat, but also radicalizes those groups and individuals who might have otherwise limited themselves to nonviolent means.

Despite a four-year antiterrorist campaign that has involved a suspension of basic freedoms and an expansion of law enforcement's powers, terrorism has persisted in Chechnya. Such an approach can check terrorism in the region in the short-term, but cannot provide a long-term solution. Heavy-handed methods of suppression could backfire because they generate resentment and turn people to extremist ideologies. Some corrupt law-enforcement officials are sympathetic to terrorists and other extremist groups, such as skinheads, which exacerbates the problem.

Repressive methods in Chechnya, coupled with law enforcement's enhanced powers, have led to the proliferation of terrorist networks in neighboring areas of the North Caucasus. Terrorists' search for allies has been the most intensive in Dagestan, which is second only to Chechnya in the suppression of liberties, the brutality of local authorities, and Wahhabist [fundamentalist sect of Islam] tendencies.

Moreover, in their attempts to broaden their popular support base, terrorist groups often co-opt the rhetoric of civil liberties, which devalues these concepts in the eyes of the general public.

These groups' efforts to gain recognition as freedom fighters succeeded in regions where the opposition had been driven underground. Radical groups in Chechnya and Dagestan have won support not only by criticizing the suppression of religion and other freedoms but also by pointing out specific violations, such as grossly falsified election results. These criticisms would not sway public opinion in Moscow and St. Petersburg, which fare much better than the North Caucasus in terms of oversight and the observance of rights and freedoms.

Although the law guarantees a certain degree of freedom in a region, terrorism will grow in the absence of public and official oversight of law enforcement, as is the case in Dagestan. In comparison, the regions that have relatively abundant liberties and freedoms, and robust public oversight of law enforcement, do not have endemic actors of terror, as is the case in Moscow and St. Petersburg.

Strong public oversight, however, would not be sufficient to rid these two regions of extremist groups in the absence of stringent official oversight of law-enforcement agencies. While robust public oversight can be effective in preventing and uncovering abuses by law-enforcement officials, it cannot force their inert agencies to dismantle extremist groups or to shift their focus from investigating traditional crimes to preventing terrorism. Only strong official oversight, not just by prosecutors but by the State Duma as well, can lead to such systemic change.

Nonetheless, such reform would not fully protect any region from terrorists. Terrorist groups in Russia would continue to target Moscow because they can achieve maximum impact on the government, people, and international community. . . .

Civilian Oversight and Government Transparency Is Needed

Russia can fight terrorism without suppressing individual and collective freedoms if its law-enforcement and security agencies focus their powers and resources on interdicting terrorist attacks rather than harassing groups and individuals suspected of radicalism. However, these powers and resources should not be excessive and must be clearly defined. Antiterror and security legislation should set clear limitations on these powers, as well as on authorities' responses not only to attacks but also to the threat of attack. The legislation should define threats and specify appropriate responses to each type, including the duration of the response. The more detailed the legislation, the better. Vaguely worded laws, manuals, and procedures provide plenty of opportunities for abuse by law enforcement.

In addition to clearly defined legislation, robust official and civilian oversight would not only help prevent abuses and the illegal repression of liberties, but would also impel law enforcement to be earnest and focused in its work.

Furthermore, the criteria used to evaluate the performance of law-enforcement agencies must be changed. As of 2005, these evaluations were largely based on crime-solving rates, encouraging officers to cover-up crimes and abuse suspects to extract confessions. The performance of law-enforcement agencies engaged in fighting terror should be evaluated on their ability to stop attackers rather than punish them.

Finally, these changes will not be comprehensive or enjoy popular support if they are not transparent. Only if they are debated by the expert community and society at large, before being codified as law, will these reforms be effective, fair, and supported by the general public.

Periodical Bibliography

The following articles have been selected to supplement the diverse views presented in this chapter.

Anne Applebaum   "Putin's Potemkin Democracy: Why Does Russia Bother to Hold Elections?" *Slate*, March 3, 2008. www.slate.com.

Mike Eckel   "Russian Extremism Law Casts Wide Net," *Washington Post*, September 3, 2007.

Economist   "Putin's People," August 23, 2007.

Mikhail Gorbachev   "Memo to Medvedev: Democracy Counts," *Times* (London) *Online*, March 5, 2008. www.timesonline.co.uk/tol/comment/columnists/guest_contributors/article3485394.ece.

Fiona Hill   "The Putin Era in Historical Perspective," *National Intelligence Council Reports*, (CR 2007-01), February 2007. www.dni.gov/nic/PDF_GIF_confreports/putin_era.pdf.

Owen Matthews and Anna Nemtsova   "Beating Down Democracy," *Newsweek International*, April 2007.

Michael McFaul and Kathryn Stoner-Weiss   "The Myth of the Authoritarian Model: How Putin's Crackdown Holds Russia Back," *Foreign Affairs*, January–February 2008.

Sarah E. Mendelson   "Dreaming of a Democratic Russia," *American Scholar*, Spring 2008.

Andrew Nagorski   "The New Cold Warrior," *Newsweek*, February 15, 2008.

The Other Russia   "Russian Opposition Discusses New Partnership," January 27, 2008. www.theotherrussia.org.

Ellen Ratner   "From Russia with Polonium 210?" *WorldNetDaily*, November 27, 2006. www.worldnetdaily.com.

CHAPTER 3

How Is Western Culture
Influencing Russia?

Chapter Preface

In August 2007, *Moscow News* interviewer Dmitry Bulin complained that "in the past few years there has been much hand-wringing about the pervasiveness of Western culture in Russia: Western TV shows and films, the propaganda of the Western lifestyle, values, and its worldview. Thus far, there has been much talk but little action on the issue." Many observers of Russian president Vladimir Putin (who was succeeded by Dmitry Medvedev, from the same party, in 2008) would disagree with Bulin's conclusion. Subtly and not so subtly, during his eight-year administration Putin set out to foster Russian patriotism, restore Russians' pride in their culture and history, and redefine Russian identity in what has been characterized as a deliberate effort to counter Western influence and reshape the Russian mind.

Some of Putin's initiatives have been welcomed as cross-cultural bridges. In 2007, for example, Putin issued a decree establishing the Russian World Foundation, or Russkiy Mir, to disseminate and promote Russian culture and the speaking and study of the Russian language abroad. In the early twentieth century, the foundation notes, one in eight people on the planet lived on the territory of the Russian Empire; today, one in fifty people resides in Russia. The foundation's mission is to keep a sense of Russian kinship alive in all people with Russian backgrounds, and to sponsor online projects and cultural events that educate non-Russians about Russian arts, literature, science, and history.

Other signs have puzzled analysts and prompted concern about their larger implications. One is the way Putin advances the concept of "the Russian people" in his political speech. There are two words in the Russian language that mean "Russians:" *Russkiy*, which refers to ethnicity and language, and *Rossiiskiy*, which refers to geographical Russia. Putin's predecessor, Boris Yeltsin, always identified Russians in territorial terms, as *Rossiiskiy*, or citizens of the Russian state. But Putin uses the word *Russkiy* as, according to Russian Academy of Sciences professor Valery Tishkov, "a historical category ('the Russian people have for centuries remained silent'), as an analogy of the Soviet people ('the breakup of the Soviet Union became a real drama for the Russian people'), and as the contemporary 'people of Russia.'" Analysts wonder if this deliberate usage signifies not just Putin's benign wish to improve relations between Russia's many ethnic minorities by emphasizing what they share, but also the implication that all former Soviet peoples are in some sense Russian and therefore under Russian control.

Finally, one aspect of Putin's ambitious efforts to boost Russian pride and patriotism has drawn not just concern but sharp disapproval inside and outside Russia. That is the apparent effort to rewrite the record and rehabilitate the reputation of Soviet dictator Joseph Stalin, whose twenty-six-year regime (1927–1953) is widely regarded as one of the most brutal and repressive in history. Under Stalin, an estimated ten million people were executed for political or criminal offenses, died in Siberian forced-labor camps, or perished in famines directly attributable to Stalin's rigid economic policies. Now, however, the Russian Academy of Education is revising key history textbooks to omit that information (one now refers to Stalin simply as "the most successful leader of the USSR") and Russian teachers are encouraged to make their pupils "proud of their motherland." According to *Newsweek* reporter Owen Matthews, Putin aims to "whitewash the atrocities committed by Stalin and downplay the Soviet Union's loss of the cold war." Putin himself "told a conference of history teachers . . . that Russia 'has nothing to be ashamed of' and that it was time to 'stop apologizing.'"

The viewpoints in this chapter consider several other ways in which Russia is responding to Western influences and reasserting its own identity.

> "The Russian consumer market doubled in the past ten years. Analysts say it will double again in just the next five years."

Western Consumer Goods Are Improving Russians' Standard of Living

Steve Liesman

In the following viewpoint, Steve Liesman describes the boom in consumerism and the rise of Western retailers in Russia since 2000. Western automobiles, electronics, clothing brands, and household furnishings and appliances are all in high demand, and retailers such as Ikea are reporting sales increases of 20 percent per year in the Russian market. Remarkably, Liesman says, the buying spree is being financed almost entirely by cash, as Russian consumers both enjoy increasing levels of disposable income and maintain their traditional aversion to debt and credit purchases. Steve Liesman is an economics reporter for the business news network CNBC.

As you read, consider the following questions:

1. Why do Russians have so much more money to spend on consumer goods, according to Liesman?

2. In what ways are Russian shopping preferences different from those of their Western counterparts, according to the author? In what ways are they similar?

3. What is the average debt per capita in Russia, according to Renaissance Capital's Roland Nash, cited by the author?

Wall units, bunk beds and lamps—a Russian consumer boom has meant plenty of normal sales for the Ikea store in Moscow.

But shopping carts are also filled with some unusual items, such as white New Zealand sheepskins and mosquito netting.

"You know that is a gadget for small teen girls, normally. Suddenly we have sold more of these nets in Russia than all of Ikea together," said Lennart Dahlgren, general manager of Ikea Russia.

A Booming Consumer Market

Dahlgren, Ikea's man in Russia, doesn't know—or even care—why Russians covet these items.

What he does know is that sales are 20 percent ahead of last year as the company has adapted to a peculiar but surging Russian consumer market. And he is extremely bullish when it comes to Russia's potential. "Without limits, without limits. When I say 'without limits' it is for us. We can make two Ikea stores a year and we will never reach the limits," Dahlgren said.

Al Breach, the chief economist and strategist at [investment bank] Brunswick UBS, said money is being pumped into the economy. "[There's] a huge amount of free cash flow . . . huge amount of wealth being generated in cash and people are starting to spend it and enjoy it."

Russian incomes have surged with the booming Russian economy. Russians now have money to buy the latest goods, from the latest electronics to washing machines. Foreign products are flying off the shelves.

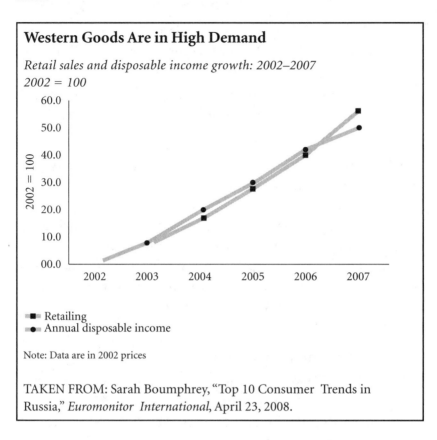

Western Goods Are in High Demand

Retail sales and disposable income growth: 2002–2007
2002 = 100

- ■ Retailing
- ● Annual disposable income

Note: Data are in 2002 prices

TAKEN FROM: Sarah Boumphrey, "Top 10 Consumer Trends in Russia," *Euromonitor International*, April 23, 2008.

"Compared with five years ago, two or three times the amount of people are buying more expensive technology," said appliance salesman Roman Yudin.

The Russian consumer market doubled in the past ten years. Analysts say it will double again in just the next five years.

Why Can Russians Now Afford to Buy More?

The wellsprings of retail are oil dollars and low living expenses. Privatization of apartments at moderate prices has given Russians relatively low housing costs. And Russian [former] President Vladimir Putin slashed taxes to just 13 percent, putting more rubles in Russians' pockets. "Russians, you know, being dressy and liking to look nice . . . tend to spend a much higher percentage of their income on makeup and clothes," said *Cosmopolitan Russia* Editor Elena Nyasnikova. Disposable income, adjusted for inflation, has grown a stunning 9 percent for each of the past three years.

Adjusting Western-Style Sales Practices

But western sales practices have not always translated well in Russia.

For example, one Audi dealership's sales have doubled every year for the past four years, but it found a cultural problem offering western-style service. "Now, we tell our guys to say hello to people," said Audi salesman Matt Donnelly. "So they walk in and say 'hello' and they go, 'Wow! What do you want? Leave me alone!'"

But in some ways, Russian consumers are just like their western counterparts. They love shopping in malls. "I like it because everything is all at one place, very comfortable," said Elena Zatchcova, a Russian shopper. "[There are] a lot of stores, there is food here so you can spend the whole day here. There is parking . . . it is very convenient."

The Mega Mall was built and financed by furniture giant Ikea, and offers over 2 million square feet of retail bliss for eager Russian shoppers. This year alone, they expect over 40 million customers.

That would make it the most heavily trafficked mall in all of Europe.

Expanding the Market

But such malls remain the exception. Many Russians still shop in open-air bazaars. And others lack the incomes to partake in the consumer boom.

But for all their shopping, one thing is missing in Russia: credit. Almost all transactions are in cash. Russian consumers carry almost no debt.

Not yet, anyway.

"Debt per capita in Russia, including mortgages and consumer credit, is about $20 per head," said [Russian investment bank] Renaissance Capital's Roland Nash. "In the U.S., it's $20,000 per head."

Much of the consumerism in Russia is taking place in the major cities, but many companies consider the outer regions of the country as the biggest growth opportunity.

> "Millions of Russians . . . can act like the professional consumers they've always dreamed of becoming. So what if they're signing themselves up for debt serfdom? Americans do it."

Western-Style Consumer Credit Is Driving Russians into Debt

Yasha Levine

In the following viewpoint, Yasha Levine warns that the Russian buying spree, fueled by easy credit and an influx of Western consumer goods, has a dark downside. According to Levine, Russia's banking industry is "bringing the consumer credit market to the brink" by such practices as handing out loans to people with virtually no credit checks, charging exorbitant interest rates, and failing to establish a centralized credit bureau. That's why "Russia's debtors are defaulting on roughly 35% of outstanding loans," and, Levine worries, if the default rate is this high at "the peak of a huge economic boom, then what will happen if the economy takes a turn?" Yasha Levine is an editor at The eXile, *a*

Moscow-based, English-language newspaper popular among Moscow's expatriate community for satirical and serious investigative journalism and irreverent critiques of life in modern Russia.

As you read, consider the following questions:

1. What was Russia's total consumer debt in 2004, according to Levine? What was the total consumer debt in 2006?

2. What information does the bank Russkiy Standart require to approve a loan of $10,000, according to the author?

3. According to Garry Kasparov, quoted by the author, 85 percent of the Russian people are not benefiting from the flow of petrodollars into Russia's economy. How does the "E-Z credit economy" mask this problem, in Levine's view?

The greatest threat to [the former president Vladimir] Putin regime isn't what's grabbing all the headlines—opposition marches, NATO encirclement, separatism in the Caucasus, the ever-crumbling infrastructure. No, the most likely threat to stability comes from a more obvious yet far less sexy source: E-Z consumer credit. . . .

Just two years ago, consumer credit was still relatively new and rare in Russia. Sure, loans have been available for years, but until recently banks weren't as eager to issue consumer credit as easily as they do now, and Russians weren't lining up in droves to finance a rabidly consumerist lifestyle. But, oh, how that's changed.

Skyrocketing Loans

In 2004, Russia's total consumer loans amounted to about $20 billion. Two years later, that number quadrupled, or more. At the end of 2006, consumer debt hovered just below the $80 billion mark (about 8% of Russia's GDP [gross domestic product]), according to Alfa Bank. If you listen to Russia's Central Bank (CBR), the number was closer to $100 billion.

The 400% jump in Russia's personal credit revolution was not the result of a decision by the CBR to stimulate the economy by lowering interest rates. In fact, in the two-year period, interloan interest rates (the rates at which banks loan money to each other) rose by a few percentage points. This bubble wasn't caused by fiscal policy, but by speculation and greed.

Skyrocketing Loan Defaults and Loan-Shark Interest Rates

According to the Russian daily *Kommersant*, Russian debtors are defaulting on roughly 35% of outstanding loans. You read that right. Thirty-five percent. This figure should have the financial sector . . . transferring its money into [gold] bullion. In comparison, only 5% of all American mortgages were foreclosed in 2006. But the *Kommersant* article, published [in early 2007] didn't cause any waves.

Home Bank, a small Russian subsidiary of a Czech bank called Home Credit and Finance Bank, is a shining example of the type of institution that's bringing the consumer credit market to the brink. According to *PROFIL* magazine, Home takes pride in the fact that the bank approves virtually anyone with a heartbeat. As a result, Home proudly posts a whopping 22% default rate on their loans. That's right, nearly one out of every four people borrowing money from them couldn't pay them back. But the bank isn't worried. They sell their bad debt to collection agencies for pennies on the dollar and still make enough to turn a handsome profit. The trick to the whole industry lies in the exorbitant interest rates they charge those who don't welch; the losses are more than covered by the people that manage to pay off their loans. The result is a classic pyramid scheme.

The banking industry is loathe to admit this, but Home's practices are the industry standard. To see if Russian banks are indeed as suicidal as they're made out to be, the *eXile* called Russia's five largest banks to find out what it takes to get $10,000 in cash, no questions asked.

Turns out, credit history is not even a factor in the decision-making process. In the 16 years of Russia's market economy, no centralized credit bureau has been established. Banks compile their own credit ratings and you can get a huge credit rating database pirated from large banks at any *rynok* [market] in Moscow, but banks have yet to begin sharing the information amongst themselves.

Banks clearly aren't motivated by their clients' ability to pay off loans. Rather, they're driven by the fear that the borrower will take his business elsewhere. With the competition in mind, each bank assured us that getting a loan would not be a problem, even when we hinted that our income isn't always as regular as we'd like. All we needed, the banking reps assured us, was a valid passport, written proof of employment, and deposit slips showing income. They didn't care much about our salary, just so long as some of it was legal.

Of all the banks, Russkiy Standart was by far the most, er, generous. Russkiy Standart is Russia's largest consumer lender. For awhile, the bank gave out loans like toasters. All they required was a passport, proof that the borrower has maintained a job for at least six months and a co-signer who also had a six-month employment history. That's it. Provided that, you could walk out of a Russkiy Standart loan department with a fat stack of rubles equaling $10,000.

It's almost like free money. And it is, until you look at their jaw-smacking interest rates.

The Russian Consumer Bubble Will Burst

How long can the banks keep it going? How many dirt-poor Russian debtors can they keep shoveling off to collector agen-

Roustam Tariko: Russia's Pioneer in Consumer Credit

[Today Moscow] is marked by ostentatious displays of consumerism—billboards for Rolex and other luxury goods surround even the Kremlin—and [44-year-old Roustam] Tariko has amassed an estimated $1.9 billion fortune. . . .

Tariko made this fortune . . . by seizing on the insight that even ordinary Russians want a taste of the good life. Just as the nation began to open to the West, Tariko started importing Italian chocolates and liquor. Then, under the banner of Russian Standard Group, he created a brand of his own: the $10 Russian Standard vodka (a lot for most Muscovites). And amid the misery of the 1998 Russian banking crisis he founded Russian Standard Bank, a pioneer in consumer credit that gave millions of [Russian citizens] their first opportunity to buy dishwashers, TVs and refrigerators.

These companies have all reaped the benefits of Russia's natural resources-fueled economy, humming at 6.5% annual growth since the end of the financial crisis. Sales at Tariko's privately held import company, Roust Trading, have increased since then 27% annually to $221 million [in 2005].

Michael Freedman, "A Common Touch,"
Forbes.com, March 27, 2006.

cies before the entire Russian population has repo men stealing their cars and goons knocking down their doors and dragging out their brand new plasma TVs? If up to a third of Russians are defaulting during the peak of a huge economic boom, then what will happen if the economy takes a turn? What will happen if something like the recent China tremors or America's growing debt problems cause investors to pull money out of Russia, or oil prices to fall?

Investment banker Jim Rogers, who correctly predicted a bull market in commodities that began in 1999 and opened the massively successful Quantum Fund with George Soros, doesn't need to be told what will happen.

"I wouldn't put a nickel of my own money in Russia, and I wouldn't put a nickel of your money there either," he recently announced. "Everything about Russia is one big bubble, and it's going to pop. It's going to happen sooner rather than later.... When that happens, people will look around and say, how did that happen? That's when we'll find out about all the skeletons in the cupboard," Rogers told Reuters [news service] in a ranting telephone interview [in May 2007.]

According to him, the slightest glitch in Russia's economy and the whole thing could tumble like a house of cards. But not everyone agrees.

Easy Credit Makes Russians Less Likely to Criticize the Government

Our source at Alpha Bank thinks it's all hype. According to her, Russia's credit and real estate markets aren't as fluid as Western markets. Russia's low consumer debt/GDP [gross domestic product] ratio (currently at 8%, as opposed to America's 92%) is going to limit the fallout of any banking shocks, and shield the country's real estate markets....

Is it too late to prevent the meltdown? The only thing that could help now would be for the federal government to start pumping money into the banking system so the banks can start lowering interest rates. It looks like this might be happening as well. The average interbank loan rate in 2007 is already 2% lower than the average of the last quarter of 2006.

If the credit economy were to crash, you might start to see a lot more people with the time and energy to protest. Because if there's one thing that can crush the opposition more completely than censorship, jail time and OMON [special units of the Russian police] put together, it's Russia's new E-Z credit economy. If there's one thing that can make living in an FSB [Russia's secret service]-controlled state tolerable, it's free money of the sort we've been seeing.

The protest leaders don't seem to grasp this. "When 85% of this country's population isn't seeing the benefits brought in by the flow of petrodollars, a new team must analyze this horrible social layering," Garry Kasparov [a prominent critic of Putin's] told Russian *Newsweek* after the protest.

But easy consumer credit is doing a pretty good job of temporarily masking this "horrible social layering." Who needs a thriving and growing middle class when even Russia's poorest village dwellers can go on the biggest shopping spree of their lives, paid for with someone else's—a bank's, that is—credit? Why waste your day protesting in the streets and run the risk of getting billy-clubbed and thrown in jail, when you can go shopping for the newest 54-inch LCD TV with Dolby Digital surround sound and then spend the next 6 months bragging about it to your drinking buddies?

One of the main reasons behind Putin's popularity—as well as one of the reasons the opposition doesn't have a chance—is that millions of Russians, for the first time since 1991, can act like the professional consumers they've always dreamed of becoming. So what if they're signing themselves up for debt serfdom? Americans do it.

But if the credit shit hits the fan and liquidity suddenly dries up, it could be the end for Putin's New Russia, and the start of something that none of us would even dare to guess.

> "A group of 150 New Russians paid 700,000 a ticket to engage Whitney Houston, Mariah Carey and Justin Timberlake to entertain them on a flight en route to a Lord of the Rings theme party in Iceland."

Russians Embrace Western Pop Culture

Viv Groskop

In the following viewpoint, Viv Groskop discusses a trend among Russia's elite of hiring international pop stars for private parties or exclusive events. While these celebrities are mostly American, Russian pop has also been influenced by musical traditions left over from the Soviet era. Viv Groskop is a contributing writer for New Statesman.

As you read, consider the following questions:

1. How much did "Russia's richest civil servant" reportedly pay for an appearance by Christina Aguilera and Shakira?
2. Who are the *Estrada* divas, and how do they relate to the modern pop stars?

3. Who is Russia's Liza Minnelli?

With a reputation for partying almost as much as for politics, Boris Yeltsin would have rejoiced at New Russian determination to enjoy a good time at any cost. But would he have approved of the oligarch who just paid Jennifer Lopez over £1m [million] to perform at his wife's birthday party?

Hiring International Pop Stars

Andrei Melnichenko, 34, a friend of the billionaire owner of Chelsea FC Roman Abramovich, ranks at 258 in the Forbes rich list with an estimated fortune of $2.7bn [billion]: he made his money in metals, electrics, banking and fertilisers. He hired Lopez to sing for 40 minutes—£600,000 for the set, £400,000 for her entourage—at a lavish party in the Berkshire countryside [in 2007] to celebrate the 30th birthday of his wife, Aleksandra, a Serbian former model (with a passing resemblance to La Lopez). Lopez and co were put up in a London hotel.

Hiring international pop stars for top dollar has become something of a trend in Russia's smartest set. For his wedding in 2005, Melnichenko secured Whitney Houston, Christina Aguilera and, perhaps less groovily, Julio and Enrique Iglesias. Not to be outdone, in March [2006] the oligarch playboy Suleiman Kerimov—number 72 on the Forbes rich list and dubbed "Russia's richest civil servant"—paid a reported £580,000 each to Christina Aguilera and Shakira to sing at his 40th birthday party in Moscow.

Komsomolskaya Pravda reported that [New Year's Eve 2007] a group of 150 New Russians paid 700,000 a ticket to engage Whitney Houston, Mariah Carey and Justin Timberlake to entertain them on a flight en route to a *Lord of the Rings* theme party in Iceland. Mariah Carey, it is reported, has been repeatedly courted by an unnamed oligarch, who keeps sending her £5,000 fur coats (which are rejected as she is an animal rights supporter).

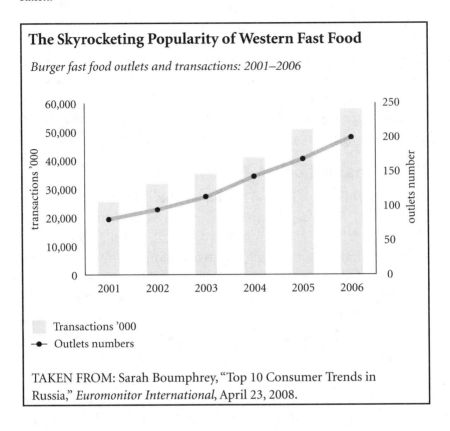

The Skyrocketing Popularity of Western Fast Food

Burger fast food outlets and transactions: 2001–2006

Transactions '000
—●— Outlets numbers

TAKEN FROM: Sarah Boumphrey, "Top 10 Consumer Trends in Russia," *Euromonitor International*, April 23, 2008.

Traditional Influences in Pop Culture

The oligarchs' choice of entertainers—divas, in the main, with big voices and even bigger hair—is not surprising. Super-cool New Russians may not like to be reminded, but their tastes have their origins in "estrada", a Soviet musical tradition that had its heyday in the 1980s.

Estrada divas are Soviet Shakiras: larger than life, in sequins and feathers, with a huge vocal range and the capacity to reduce a red-blooded Russian man to tears.

The queen of the genre, Alla Pugacheva, dubbed Russia's Liza Minnelli, is still going strong after 30 years in the business and has her own shoe and perfume lines. She is so popular that when Russia entered the Eurovision Song Contest in

1997, most people assumed that by choosing her it was a done deal. There was national outrage when she came 15th.

Estrada means "as performed on stage" and refers to the sort of ballads usually classed as musical theatre. Typical themes include falling autumn leaves, snow-bound farewells and, an Alla Pugacheva favourite, a romantic homage to Superman ("I will teach you Russian and you can teach me English. Say after me: balalaika.") *Estrada* may be old-fashioned, but Putin has often said he is a fan and it still occupies a Saturday night slot on state television.

Which is perhaps why US divas like J-Lo have crowded out home-grown stars at all the oligarchs' parties. Why pay for something you can get for free on prime-time TV? A socialist and a pragmatist, Yeltsin would, one suspects, have rather watched his Russian favourites for nothing.

> "*Priority is given to all things Russian. . . . You may call it propaganda, but we need to stop this tendency to beat ourselves up, stop selling out our country.*"

Russians Embrace Patriotic Homegrown Culture

Fred Weir

In the following viewpoint, Fred Weir describes a range of initiatives that aim to wean the Russian people away from Western-style entertainment and fashions and strengthen their support of Russian traditions and the Russian government. These initiatives are funded by the Putin-endorsed Russian World Foundation, an organization dedicated to the development, promotion, and dissemination of Russian culture and language at home and abroad. The foundation, Weir reports, is part of a resurgence of patriotism and cultural nationalism in Russia that is part backlash against pervasive Western cultural influences and part state-sponsored project to strengthen conservative political policies and foster Russian pride and identity. Fred Weir is a correspondent for The Christian Science Monitor.

As you read, consider the following questions:

1. What is Zvezda and what does it do, according to Weir?

2. Who does the author say will receive state subsidies for introducing "themes of national pride" into their work?

3. What is Russia Today and what does it do, according to the author?

Islamic bandits. Sandstorms. A Red Army officer fighting venal bureaucrats to bring Communism to the wilds of Central Asia, liberate Muslim women from their veils, and spread the light of Soviet power.

It's *White Sun of the Desert*, and just about every Russian has seen this 1960s film. Even now when it comes on TV, people drop everything to watch it.

This feel-good homegrown Russian flick is a nostalgic return to a time when Russian society radiated a collective purpose and national determination, one that has been beaten down since the collapse of the Soviet Union [in 1991]. Movies like *White Sun* serve as ballast for a society overrun by Western fare like *Sex and the City*, *Alien Resurrection*, and *Doc Hollywood*. And if Ivan Kononov has his way, it's the kind of programming that will help revive the traditional my-country-first patriotism that guided Russians for centuries and led to great triumphs in war, culture, and science.

Government Initiatives Focus on Russian Culture

Mr. Kononov is a top producer at Zvezda, a newly-launched state-run TV network. Zvezda, which means "star," is one of several government-funded initiatives ostensibly aimed at correcting what the Kremlin perceives is a dearth of national pride and identification with the state—especially among Russia's rudderless youth. "Until now, there is not a single TV channel oriented on the ideas of the Fatherland where priority is given to all things Russian," Kononov says. "You may call it

Natasha and Dima, the Russian Barbie and Ken

The [Russian] government answer to Barbie, Ken, and their assorted paraphernalia, has been Natasha and Dima. Boris Bukharov, Deputy Director of Science at the Moscow Institute of Toys, said: "They were recently put into production, along with a daughter, a friend and a complete set of furniture." . . .

Natasha and Dima are the latest in a long series of Russian replacements for their popular Western counterparts. . . .

The Kremlin has recently tried to extend its control over other fields of Russian entertainment, the Ministry of Culture announcing that vital state funding would be given in preference to films of a patriotic nature.

Nick Paton Walsh,
"Barbie Is Banned from Russia, Without Love,"
Observer, *November 24, 2002.*

propaganda, but we need to stop this tendency to beat ourselves up, stop selling out our country."

Zvezda, which kicked off in March [2005] and currently reaches about 50 million Russian households, so far spends most of its 24-hour cycle showing Soviet films, plus a few military documentaries and interviews with notable Russians. Kononov says programming will soon expand to include talk shows and open forums for young people to discuss their "burning questions," particularly the widespread aversion to military service.

[In July 2005] the Kremlin signed off on an ambitious five-year program, involving 22 government ministries, to buck up Russia's image at home and abroad as well as unspecified, but potentially ominous, efforts to "resist attempts to discredit and devalue patriotic ideas in the media, literature, and the arts." In addition to Zvezda, state subsidies will be offered to artists, journalists, and educators for introducing themes of national pride into their work, software experts will be hired to develop patriotic computer games and, for the first time since the Soviet era, schoolchildren will be required to take rudimentary military and civil defense training.

Also projected are steps to correct the allegedly false image of Russia held by many in the outside world, which Kremlin officials have often suggested is the work of "anti-Russian" and "cold-war minded" foreign journalists. A $30 million English-language, 24-hour satellite news channel called Russia Today will be launched later this year by the state-run RIA-Novosti news agency, to bring the "positive news" about Russia to the world. "I frequently watch the foreign television channels, and almost everywhere they are saying the same things [about Russia]," President Vladimir Putin told leaders of the Kremlin-sponsored patriotic youth group Nashi [in August 2005]. "All they can talk about is crisis and breakdown."

Restoring Respect for Russian Institutions

Critics say the Kremlin's patriotism project is little more than an expensive PR offensive to paper over Russia's very real problems, particularly the state of the military. Zvezda, funded mainly by the Defense Ministry, is an attempt to stem the tide of draft evasion—only 11 percent of eligible young men were conscripted [in 2004]—by presenting a rosy view of Army life, they say. "This is just a bureaucratic approach that smells of Soviet methods," says Vitaly Shlykov, a former Soviet official. "They have failed in all attempts to actually reform the Army, so now they've decided to teach patriotism instead."

Some wonder why Russia, which already has three nationwide state-controlled TV networks, needs any new ones. News broadcasts on the big three already hew the Kremlin line and have sharply increased patriotic programming, including popular new films and miniseries such as *Soldiers*, *National Security Agent*, and *The Motherland is Waiting*, that glorify military and state service.

But Kononov says Russia's existing channels have become hopelessly commercialized and addicted to Western-style entertainment. "Sure, they have some patriotic programming, but they mainly broadcast shows about crime, political scandal, and foreign films," he says. "There is little about them that can be called Russian."

Vladimir Pozner, host of a top-rated public-affairs TV program, says Kononov's concerns are widely shared. "There's no doubt that younger people today lack respect for Russia's institutions, that the sense of pride and love for one's country is at low ebb," he says. "But how do you teach patriotic feelings?"

He is even more critical of Russia Today's goal of remaking world opinion. "The negative image of Russia in the West today comes from what's happening inside Russia," he says. "We know from past experience that until we start changing ourselves in positive ways, we won't be able to do much about the way others view us."

> *"Many westerners who have entrepreneurial skills . . . say that Russia became the land of opportunity several years ago."*

Westerners Want to Work and Live in Russia

Olga Sharapova

In the following viewpoint, Russian journalist Olga Sharapova counters a common perception among ordinary Russians that life is better in the West with evidence that Westerners would rather work and live in Russia. Attracted by business opportunity, low taxes, and resources "from newspapers to schools, art festivals to ethnic restaurants," she says, Westerners come to work, study, or travel and end up settling across the country as far as Siberia, no longer concentrated in the urban centers of Moscow and St. Petersburg. Olga Sharapova is a contributor to Russian Times *magazine and special correspondent for the* St. Petersburg Times *weekly newspaper.*

Olga Sharapova, "The Attraction of Mother Russia," *St. Petersburg Times,* March 25, 2008. Copyright © 1993 - 2008 The St. Petersburg Times. Reproduced by permission.

As you read, consider the following questions:

1. What factors have created a good business climate for Westerners in Russia, according to business consultant Yury Mikhailov and manager Svetlana Sokhatskaya, quoted by the author?

2. What Russian industries are attracting the most Western investment, according to Sharapova?

3. What does Sharapova say are the most popular jobs for Western expatriates in Russia?

When Peter the Great started building St. Petersburg in 1703, his vision was of a new capital that would resemble a western city in both appearance and customs. With impressive energy and entrepreneurial skills, Peter I tried to bring the best European achievements to Russia, such as business knowledge, practicality, good organization and attention to education, arts and science.

But even today, few Russians identify their homeland as a completely European country. There are many historical, political and cultural reasons for this—not least that it needs more time to integrate the Russian economy into international business processes than the . . . years that have passed since the break-up of the Soviet Union [in 1991].

Russia Has Become the "Land of Opportunity"

Step by step however, Russia is becoming an increasingly open country. Foreigners come to live in Russia for various reasons, such as to do business, study or work in the diplomatic service. Naturally, they bring with them their own cultures, experiences and habits. Moscow and St. Petersburg, where most expatriates [or "ex-pats," citizens who choose to live abroad] in Russia are based, now offer considerable resources for foreign communities, from newspapers to schools, art festivals to ethnic restaurants and much more. Successful westerners may also unintentionally enhance the very popular idea among Russians that life in the West is completely different and far easier than in Russia.

According to the Russian mentality—or rather the Soviet way of thinking that is still alive in most adult Russians—wealthy foreign countries seem to many Russians to be the best places in the world. In the words of Arjen Roodvoets, a Dutch citizen who teaches his native language to Russians at both St. Petersburg State University and the Netherlands Institute, "Russians often think that life in the West is much better than here, but it is often not true. There is also an understated self-appreciation in Russia. In my opinion, Russia is a really special and original country. Russians should just be who they are, be natural and maintain their native values, such as a strong education system and culture."

Roodvoets, who has lived and worked in Russia for nine years, has become deeply involved in Russian society and has adapted to Russian life. "I like many things in Russia, enjoy the Russian language and dealing with local people. One of the best things is my job here, because I like communicating with Russians." Roodvoets, who speaks fluent Russian, was baptized in Russia and his favorite place in St. Petersburg is Valaamskoe Podvorie church on Staropetergovski prospekt.

"I think it is Orthodoxy that distinguishes Russia from other European countries and has formed the national mentality," he says.

Two-Way Cultural Exchange

The cultural exchange between Russians and ex-pats is a two-way process. It is generally accepted that many aspects of Russian life have been westernized in a positive way (primarily business and management), and it is also true that there are a number of foreigners who enjoy exploring the differences between their own lifestyle and life in Russia.

Russian Emigrants Are Returning to Russia

Repatriates, or repats as they're more usually known—Russian nationals who emigrated some time ago, and who are now returning in larger numbers than ever before—are being very proactively sought out by headhunters. Faced with an increasingly competitive fight for local talent, recruitment firms who have global reach through large office networks are now increasingly being asked to search internationally for Russian nationals. . . .

One major reason why repats are open to the idea of moving back to Russia is that, despite the fact that Moscow has made the headlines for being one of the most expensive cities in the world, it's actually not. For the vast majority of Muscovites who shop at Auchan, eat 180-ruble ($7) set-menu lunches and grow vegetables at their dacha, the idea that it's impossible to live more cheaply in Moscow than in London or Tokyo is simply preposterous.

As for the interval between promotions, 18 months appears to be the norm.

Tremayne Elson, "Brain Drain Reversal: Repats Welcome,"
St. Petersburg Times, *October 30, 2007. www.sptimes.ru.*

Cobus van Rooijen, group sales and distribution director for Heineken Russia, says, "In my free time I usually explore cultural and natural attractions—recently, for example, I went hunting near Lake Baikal in temperatures of -35 degrees Celsius, and also attended a magnificent performance of "The Nutcracker" directed by Alexei Ratmansky at the Mariinsky theater."

Yury Mikhailov, managing partner at Consort Consulting Group, has considerable experience interacting with westerners and says he even knows some ex-pats who have become more Russian than Russians themselves by studying its history, literature, politics and character traits.

Generally, however, Mikhailov believes that "Most foreigners stay the same by going to their ex-pat bars, restaurants, clubs and consular events. This of course does not allow them to integrate and become familiar with local life."

As to the differences between Russians and westerners, in Mikhailov's opinion, "Foreigners often seek to achieve more recognition in professional circles as well as in their personal relationships."

Walter Ragonese, who is from the U.S. and works in Russia as the security and business continuity managing director of InterComp, concurs: "Most of the ex-pats I know have very fulfilling professional and social lives in Russia. Work is generally the focus of the professional/social life balance, but family and friendships are usually very significant factors in making the experience well rounded and personally satisfying."

Ragonese's colleague, Daniel J. Hill, who is general manager of InterComp Outsourcing in Russia, explains, "After 14 years in Russia, I am still here because I still find it an exciting, vibrant and dynamic place in which to work and live. I think many westerners (myself included) try to find a balance between maintaining ties with their home culture and friends, and embracing all of the new and interesting aspects of developing Russian friends and experiencing Russian culture."

Asked what inspires foreigners to come here, Ragonese says, "Moscow and St. Petersburg in particular are very cosmopolitan and attractive locations that rank alongside other cities around the world for expatriates looking to develop their careers.

"Russia has always been open to the employment of westerners who have the necessary skills required by an organization," he adds. "This hasn't changed from 16 years ago when I first arrived in Russia. Obviously the required skills have become more specific with every year as the Russian market for management talent has become more developed."

A Good Business Climate

A good investment climate and very good corporate career opportunities are among the most positive factors about working in Russia, according to [van Rooijen of Heineken Russia]. But he cited the common problem often complained about by foreigners—elements of bureaucracy. His words were echoed by Consort Consulting Group's Mikhailov: "Of course there is a certain amount of legal issues and bureaucracy, and dealing with red tape has never been easy, but it is a much more achievable goal than it used to be." He adds, "If you just think for a minute, it's not that easy to settle and work in other parts of the world unless you are an EU [European Union] citizen wanting to work in other EU countries."

From Mikhailov's diverse professional experiences, he knows that many westerners who have entrepreneurial skills and an aptitude for business say that Russia became the land of opportunity several years ago. On the issue of why Russia has become a popular country in which to work, he says, "Profitability rates and sales turnover growth are much higher here than in the west, and this is what attracts businessmen seeking a faster return on their initial investments."

Svetlana Sokhatskaya, branch manager of Kelly Services St. Petersburg, suggests that "Foreigners, in most cases, know how to count money and they realize that taxes in Russia are much lower. Many companies provide top managers from other countries with free apartments while they are working in Russia and it is, no doubt, a great advantage for westerners."

Now there is a general tendency among local firms to invite foreign managers in to make the business more efficient. "It just means," continues Sokhatskaya, "that in comparison with Russian specialists, westerners possess more international experience in business and management."

The most popular and attractive segments of the local market for foreign investment are construction, real estate, the automotive industry, IT [information technology], the hospitality industry, publishing, food and the sale of different kinds of equipment. According to Mikhailov, "The number of companies is increasing every year. Since we work closely with Finnish companies, we know that there are more than 400 Finnish firms on the local market."

InterComp's Ragonese considers that "The most popular spheres of employment for ex-pats are auditing services, taxation consulting, and law firms. Real estate consultancy and management also employ a significant number of expatriates."

One of the most dynamic industry segments is IT—virtually all the major brands are in St. Petersburg now, including Alcatel-Lucent, EMC, Motorola, Nokia, Microsoft, Google, Sun Microsystems and Intel.

The latest International Technical Exhibition at Lenexpo illustrated the level of interest in the Russian market—there were more than 100 companies from India alone at the fair, which focused on metallurgy and mechanical engineering, illustrating the line of business cooperation that Indian companies are planning to take in the near future.

Similarities of Daily Life

The profitable hospitality industry, specifically the restaurant business and tourism, also tend to attract foreign managers. A myriad of different cuisines are on offer in [St. Petersburg]—not just the usual Italian and French restaurants, but also Greek, Indian, Thai, Mexican, Korean, and many more. However, the active international presence on this business scene in turn spurs on Russians to increase their activity on the market and attract ex-pats and tourists to visit different Russian restaurants and clubs.

The private and daily lives of ex-pats in Russia may not differ greatly in some respects from the experiences of ex-pats in other foreign countries. But every country has its customs and idiosyncrasies. Van Rooijen of Heineken Russia thinks that foreigners here have several dreams—to learn the Russian language, to understand local customs and traditions, and to enjoy support in their business initiatives.

"What westerners lack in Russia," says Mikhailov of Consort Consulting Group, "is the greater sense of security and stability that they have become so attached to back home— that's why from time to time they tend to take off and head home for a couple of months to recharge their batteries, touch base with their friends and relatives, and share their Russian experiences."

InterComp's Ragonese has a keen interest in outdoor activities, and therefore lives outside the city and commutes to work every day. The most negative aspects of Russia, in his opinion, are corruption among local officials (especially the traffic police) and the aggressive behavior that Russians can display in public, even with total strangers.

But locals should not feel offended—it's not so bad to know that westerners feel the same as Russians when the latter curse their country's poor roads, corruption and impoliteness.

> *"The CIS region, especially Russia, Ukraine, and Kazakhstan, have suffered serious losses due to outflow of highly skilled professionals. . . . For Russia, the UNDP estimates annual losses resulting from brain drain as 25 billion $US."*

Russians and Migrant Workers Want to Leave Russia to Work and Live in the West

Irina Ivakhnyuk

In the following viewpoint, Irina Ivakhnyuk argues that although Russia is a net recipient of immigrants, it is mainly a sending country: educated Russian emigrants are leaving for the developed countries of the West, and the wide range of nationals from Asia, Africa, and the former Soviet republics who migrate to Russia view it as a staging point, as a place to earn money or obtain documents that will enable them to move on to better jobs and lives in Europe. Those who stay, Ivakhnyuk maintains, are stuck: unwilling to integrate with local Russian society, they

Irina Ivakhnyuk, *International Symposium on International Migration and Development, Population Division, Department of Economic and Social Affairs,* New York, NY: United Nations Secretariat, Turin, Italy, 2006. Copyright © 2006 United Nations. Reprinted with the permission of the United Nations.

send the bulk of their income out of Russia in the form of remittances to relatives back home and form a shadow economy unentitled to social benefits in Russia. Irina Ivakhnyuk is a professor of economics at Lomonosov Moscow State University and an expert on transit migration through Russia.

As you read, consider the following questions:

1. What were the primary causes of Russian immigration fifteen years ago, and what are they today, according to Ivakhnyuk?
2. How many "transit migrants" are currently stranded in Russia, according to the author?
3. According to the author, what four measures is the Russian government taking in hopes of reversing the "brain drain"?

The Commonwealth of Independent States (CIS) is a regional structure [of twelve members comprising all the post-Soviet states except the three Baltic countries], which evolved after the [Soviet Union] dissolution. In terms of migration processes, it represents a common migration system. . . .

Migration Flows In and Out of Russia

The scale of international migration within the frames of Eurasian migration system characterizes it as one of the world's biggest migration systems. The UN [United Nations] estimate (2005) ranks Russia—the major destination country in the region—the second in the list of the countries with biggest numbers of immigrants after the USA, and [ranks] Ukraine . . . the fourth . . . (USA, 38.9 million immigrants; Russia, 12.1 million; Germany, 10.1 million; Ukraine, 6.8 million).

During the last 15 years the nature of migration flows in the CIS region shifted from primarily *forced migrations*—as a result of strong political and economic push factors, such as military conflicts, social outbursts, discrimination [against] ethnic minorities, economic crisis—to voluntary *economic migrations*. Already since mid-1990s ethnic and political factors of migration were supplemented and then replaced by economic ones, both push and pull. Socio-economic differentiation among the newly sovereign states stimulated huge waves of labor migrants. Migration flows were directed primarily towards Russia, which was doing comparatively better in its transition to market economy and stabilization of socio-economic situation in comparison to most of the other CIS states. People migrate in quest of jobs, for economic and social betterment, to gain stability. . . .

For Central Asian states and Caucasus republics, Russia is the major destination country accumulating 70–90% of their labor migrants. As to Moldova and Ukraine, only about half of migrants from these countries come to Russia while the other half tends to move westward, to Europe, primarily to the Southern European countries where during the last 15 years numerous migrant networks of Moldavians and Ukrainians have been formed that provide support to the new coming countrymen and facilitate their migration.

Russia is the major receiving country in the region. However, at the same time it is a sending country: migrants from Russia move primarily to more developed western countries in Europe, South and North Americas, and Asia. . . .

Transit Migration

The post-Soviet territory is used as a transit route by migrants from Asian and even African countries wending their way to more developed countries of the European Union. According to estimates, over 300,000 transit migrants from Afghanistan, China, Angola, Pakistan, India, Sri-Lanka, Turkey, Ethiopia and other countries have got stranded in Russia and Ukraine running into an obstacle of tight control at the EU [European Union] border. They stay in Russia for months and even years (usually in illegal status) in order to raise funds for the on-ward smuggling fee or purchase of falsified travel documents and visas. They earn money in the shadow sector of economy or by criminal activities.

Numerous illegal transit migrants from remote Asian and African countries carry epidemiological risks. When staying in Russia, Ukraine or other CIS transit states they do not have proper access to a health care system.

Once in abusive situations, lack of papers and fear of arrest or deportation often prevent transit migrants from seeking help from authorities. The alternative protection frame comes from informal ethnic solidarity or criminal organizations. Therefore, illegal transit migrants can be easily recruited for crime.

Migrants in transit are not going to integrate with the local society. . . . They feel forced to stay in a country, which they regard [as] not more than a staging post on their way to more prosperous states in terms of economic opportunities and welfare system.

Meanwhile transit countries where these migrants got stuck suffer from growing shadow labor market, epidemiological risks, ethnic-based conflicts, and a bulging criminal sector of smugglers' and traffickers' services related to poorly controlled flows of transit migrants. . . .

Brain Drain

The CIS region, especially Russia, Ukraine, and Kazakhstan, have suffered serious losses due to outflow of highly skilled professionals in the 1990s. For Russia, the UNDP [United Nations Development Programme] estimates (2004) annual losses resulting from brain drain as 25 billion $US.

Researchers from former Soviet republics are working in European and American universities and research centers, pushed from their origin countries by low wages in the R&D [research and development] sector and reduced prestige of in-

Russia Has Not Halted the "Brain Drain"

Russia has lost about one-third of its scientific potential during many years of various reforms. Scientists involved in computing mathematics, genetics and biotechnologies are usually the first to leave Russia. The brain drain became especially active at the end of the 1990s, when specialists started leaving Russia in whole groups. According to expert estimates, the total number of people involved in scientific and research works halved from 1990 to 2002.

Pravda,
"With Brain Drain Declining After the Period of Perestroika, Russia's National Intellect Is Still in Danger,"
December 7, 2005. http://english.pravda.ru.

tellectual labor. Some of them have emigrated forever, while the others keep contacts with their homeland and inspire international projects, training courses, etc. for mutual benefit of researchers from CIS and other countries.

The nature of contemporary science is shifting. It is becoming more internationalized. In many fields of science, like space investigations, energy technologies, physics of high energies, molecular biology, etc., development within the frames of only one country is hardly possible now. Projects in these fields of highest priority need huge resources—human and financial. Besides, cooperation between researchers from different scientific schools gives more effective results, and 'brain exchange' is an important instrument of scientific progress and mutual enrichment of scholars. So, nowadays development of fundamental science needs global management. This means that new forms of organization and mobilization of intellectual resources at the global level are to be found. Another side of this new approach is to make the national economies able to apply and integrate the results of globally produced high technologies.

Gradually, the most advanced CIS states are coming to a new understanding that in order to participate in a newly organized global scientific research process most effectively they should not only give their brains but also be ready to absorb produced innovations in their economy. For this reason, Russia, for example, is focusing on speeding up the development of high technologies sectors (the IT [information technology] sector in Russia demonstrates the highest annual growth rate of 15%). Keeping in mind to reduce brain drain damages and to stimulate application of high technologies, Russia concentrates on (1) reorganization of R&D sector with priorities given to forward-looking studies, scientific schools, and talented young researchers; (2) restructuring of economy with special emphasis on HT [high tech] sector; (3) encouragement of private investments in R&D; (4) development of interstate cooperation in R&D sector, etc.

Migrant Remittances

Improvements in living standards of migrants' households are the most obvious positive effect of labor migration. Money earned in other countries is sent to the families that are left behind and used by migrants' households to purchase consumer goods, houses, investments in human capital and business. . . .

According to the Central Bank of Russia, the total amount of remittances sent from Russia to other CIS states increased by 7 times between 1999 and 2004: from 0.5 billion to 3.5 billion $US. According to the National Bank of Kazakhstan, since 2000 the remittances by residents and non-residents sent by official channels were growing 1.5–2 times annually, and by 2005 exceeded 1 billion $US. However, the overwhelming part of migrants' money is delivered to their origin countries not by official channels (bank transfer, postal order, other money remittance systems) but non-officially—with friends, relatives, or carried on their own. According to the Federal Migration Service of the Russian Federation, migrants take away 7–8 billion $US from Russia annually. . . .

How to Deal with Migration Problems

To maximize development-related migration benefits and minimize its negative effects, the CIS states are coming to a common understanding of necessary steps:

In the sphere of labor migration management:

- to reduce the scale of irregular migration and illegal employment by tackling the shadow sector of the economy in receiving countries; [improving] labor market regulation; and [developing] official channels of labor migration . . . in both sending and receiving countries.

In the sphere of transit migration:

- to respond to the challenges of 'asymmetric borders' by improvement of border control facilities and cooperation among the transit CIS states in immigration control; to use international instruments to reduce the risks of 'extended transit' and thousands of migrants stuck in transit countries.

In the sphere of brain drain:

- to encourage R&D sector and interstate cooperation in the field of research in order to develop knowledge-based economy and stimulate return migration of intellectuals; to initiate new organizational forms of fundamental science on supra-national level attracting necessary human and financial resources and elaboration of fair access of the countries to innovative technologies.

In the sphere of migrant remittances:

- to encourage migrants to send their remittances via official channels, and to offer incentives for migrants to invest earned money in business, human capital, local infrastructure, and development projects.

Periodical Bibliography

The following articles have been selected to supplement the diverse views presented in this chapter.

Chloe Arnold — "Is the Russian Language Dying Out in Former Soviet Republics?" *Radio Free Europe/Radio Liberty*, August 26, 2007. www.rferl.org/featuresarticle/2007/08/633CA874-92C1-411A-9753-2981492839B5.html.

Business Week — "Russia: Shoppers Gone Wild," February 20, 2006.

Mary Dejevsky — "The Restoration of Russian Pride," *Independent*, February 15, 2006.

Peter Finn — "In Russia, a Pop Culture Coup for the KGB," *Washington Post*, February 22, 2005.

Marina Lapenkova — "Hello, Can U Meet 4 Coffee ASAP 2 Discuss English Lingo, Cheers!" *Moscow News*, September 27, 2007. www.mnweekly.ru/national/20070927/55279172.html.

Owen Matthews and Anna Nemtsova — "Dumbing Russia Down," *Newsweek*, March 22, 2008.

Sonia Narang — "The Changing Face of Russia," *Frontline World*, PBS, January 30, 2007. www.pbs.org/frontlineworld/stories/russia602/additional.html.

Olga Partan — "Alla: The Jester-Queen of Russian Pop Culture," *Russian Review*, vol. 66, no. 3, July 2007.

Alex Rodriguez — "Pairing Pop Culture with Propaganda," *Chicago Tribune*, January 13, 2008.

Michael Specter — "Planet Kirsan," *New Yorker*, April 24, 2006.

Olga Yakimenko — "Tattoos Arrive," *Moscow News*, August 30, 2007. www.mnweekly.ru/culture/20070830/55271991.html.

CHAPTER 4

What Is Russia's Greatest Challenge?

Chapter Preface

Perhaps the most unusual thing about a list of Russia's most pressing problems is what is *not* on the list: climate change. As countries all over the world mobilize to assess and, if possible, avert catastrophic consequences of human-induced global warming, Russia is one of the few places in the world that actually stands to benefit. Gregg Easterbrook writes in the April 2007 *Atlantic Monthly*:

> Russia! For generations poets have bemoaned this realm as cursed by enormous, foreboding, harsh Siberia. What if the region in question were instead enormous, temperate, inviting Siberia? Climate change could place Russia in possession of the largest new region of pristine, exploitable land since the sailing ships of Europe first spied . . . North America. The snows of Siberia cover soils that have never been depleted by controlled agriculture. What's more, beneath Siberia's snow may lie geologic formations that hold vast deposits of fossil fuels, as well as mineral resources.

> When considering the ratification of the Kyoto Protocol to regulate greenhouse gases, the Moscow government dragged its feet. . . . Why might this have happened? Perhaps because Russia might be much better off in a warming world: Warming's benefits to Russia could exceed those to all other nations combined.

A look at the map supports Easterbrook's argument. Russia encircles almost half of the Arctic Ocean, where, according to U.S. Geological Survey estimates, a quarter of the world's undiscovered energy resources may lie. Although Russia's claim to half the Arctic Ocean has been rejected by the United Nations Convention on the Law of the Sea, Russia is scrambling to map the region to prove that its continental shelf indeed lies below the ocean and therefore confers ownership. If the

Arctic sea ice melts during the summer, Russia would more-over be in a prime position to control shipping on an Arctic passage, never before possible.

The implications of differential effects of global warming on international relations are enormous. Like all other countries, Russia will, of course, be involved in struggles over refugees, resources, water shortages, costs, and national borders caused by global warming. But its position is enviable, as Easterbrook explains:

> Historically privileged northern societies might not decline geopolitically, as many commentators have predicted. Indeed, the great age of northern power may lie ahead. . . . Should it turn out that headlong fossil-fuel combustion by northern nations has set in motion climate change that strengthens the world position of those same nations, future essayists will have a field day. But the prospect is serious. By the middle of the 21st century, a new global balance of power may emerge in which Russia and America are once again the world's paired superpowers—only this time during a Warming War instead of a Cold War.

The viewpoints in this chapter debate the severity and consequences of complex problems Russia *will* have to solve.

> "The demographic crisis has ... geopolitical implications. In the future, Russia, whose land makes up 30 percent of Eurasia, may simply have too few people to control its territory."

Russia Is Facing Population Decline

Victor Yasmann

In the following viewpoint, Russia analyst Victor Yasmann discusses the declining birthrate in Russia, and the intense debate around the subject. In his 2006 state-of-the-nation address, then-Russian president Vladimir Putin called population decline the most urgent problem facing Russia. His government officially predicted the population would decline from about 143 million in 2006 to between 80 and 100 million by 2050. Leading Russian sociologist Viktor Perevedentsov publicly called even this alarming forecast too optimistic. In the ensuing debate, Perevedentsov was accused of being in the pay of unnamed Western or-

Victor Yasmann, "Russia: Health Ministry Considers Solutions to Population Decline," *Radio Free Europe/Radio Liberty,* February 28, 2006. Copyright © 2006 RFE/RL, Inc. Reprinted with the permission of Radio Free Europe/Radio Liberty, 1201 Connecticut Ave., N.W. Washington DC 20036. www.rferl.org.

ganizations that wish to destroy Russia by issuing predictions of catastrophe. Yasmann is a senior regional analyst with the information service Radio Free Europe/Radio Liberty in Washington, D.C.

As you read, consider the following questions:

1. What is Russia's current population, and by how much is it shrinking each year, according to Yasmann?
2. What four factors does Yasmann cite as the primary causes of population decline in Russia?
3. Why does Health and Social Development Minister Mikhail Zurabov reject liberalization of Russia's immigration policy to address population decline, and what does he suggest should be done instead?

A dramatically declining population is one of the most acute problems facing Russia today. The country's official population, now around 143 million, is shrinking by 700,000 every year. By 2050, some experts predict that the country's population could be as low as 120 million.

The demographic crisis has not only economic, but geopolitical implications. In the future, Russia, whose land makes up 30 percent of Eurasia, may simply have too few people to control its territory.

Recently, Health and Social Development Minister Mikhail Zurabov reported to the State Duma [parliament] about the demographic crisis and what the government proposes to do about it.

Addressing the lower house of parliament on 22 February [2006], Zurabov said that Russia's population has been shrinking steadily since the beginning of the 1990s. Between 1993 and 2005, the population decreased by 4 percent, or 5.8 million people. In 2005 alone, Russia's population declined by 735,500.

Causes

The main factors contributing to the population decline are a very low birth rate, very high mortality rate, short life expectancy, and a growing number of deaths from "unnatural causes." Russia's crude death rate (the total annual number of deaths per 1,000 people) has reached 16. In comparison, the rate in the European Union [EU] is 5, in the United States 6.5, and in Japan 3.4.

Zurabov told parliament that of the over 150,000 people a year in Russia who die from "unnatural causes," 46,000 were suicides, 40,000 were killed in traffic accidents, 36,000 suffered alcohol poisoning, and 35,000 were murdered.

Zurabov also noted the high maternal mortality rate—23.4 per 100,000 mothers—and an infant mortality rate of 11 per 1,000 births, compared with 8 in the United States and 5 in the EU.

The high number of abortions carried out in Russia also contributes to the low birth rate, although this figure has declined sharply from Soviet times [the Soviet Union was disbanded in 1991]. In 2005, according to official statistics, Russian women had 1.6 million abortions, although unofficial estimates put this number as high as 4 million.

Although statistics vary, Russia's male life expectancy is around 58 years for men and 72 for women. For this reason, 30 percent of Russians—in particular men—do not reach the beginning of their pension age, Zurabov noted.

Possible Solutions?

So what can Russia do to reverse its population decline?

It looks unlikely that the phenomenon will correct itself. Russia's current birth rate of 1.34 children per woman of fertile age is considerably less than the 2.14 children required to turn around the trend. There was a brief respite in 2005, with

A Recent Rise in Russia's Birth Rate Has Not Halted Population Decline

Following the collapse of the Soviet Union, Russia's population plummeted, and until recently was shrinking at the rate of about 750,000 people a year.

So the Kremlin made kids a priority. A 2007 law expanded maternity leave benefits and payments, and granted mothers educational and other vouchers worth $10,650 for a second child and any thereafter. More important, perhaps, Russia's surging economy has made it possible for young couples to plan for their future.

The population decline hasn't halted, and demographers warn it could plummet again. But today births are on the rise, from 1.4 million in 2006 to 1.6 million in 2007— their highest level in 15 years.

"Russia Experiencing a Baby Boom,"
MSNBC.com, April 5, 2008.

an increase in the number of births. This was due to the larger number of girls born in the 1970s–1980s who were then bearing children.

Some Russian experts have suggested that the sharp depopulation is the result of the political and economic cataclysms of the 1990s. They say that liberal economic reforms were badly planned and implemented, and this led to societal insecurity and thus to families having less children.

Others have argued that Russia's decline is part of a wider trend, with even the prosperous countries of the European Union and Japan witnessing a declining birth rate and, consequentially, depopulation. Many Russian experts have stressed that the birth rate is not necessarily linked to living standards but also depends on values and societal outlook.

Some have suggested that a liberal immigration policy could address the population decline. But Zurabov, speaking to parliament, said that this proposed policy is unrealistic. Last year, he said, Russia's official migrant population increased by only 107,000—not enough to reverse the trend. The size of this migrant population is likely to be much higher, however, with some estimating that Russia could be home to 5–10 million illegal immigrants.

To cope with the depopulation, Zurabov suggested stimulating the birth rate, reducing infant mortality rates, and enhancing the reproductive health and quality of life of the population. The minister cited the Soviet experience: "In 1981–1987, the [Soviet Union] managed to get an extra 1.5 million children."

By May, Zurabov said his ministry will prepare a new demographic development concept. The document will set out national goals such as increasing the average national life expectancy and increasing the birth rate. But just how the ministry plans to do that remains unclear.

Zurabov's proposals were supported by Tatyana Yakovleva ([from the political party] Unified Russia), the chairman of the Duma health commission. She said that if Russia can reduce its deaths from cardiac and oncological diseases to EU levels, average life expectancy would rise by over 6 years. She also called for the improvement of pediatric health care and for the increase of the child-birth allowance by the end of 2006 to 10,000 rubles ($357).

Other Duma deputies were unimpressed by Zurabov's report. Vladimir Nikitin (Motherland) said that the reasons for the low birth rate and high mortality rate are identical—the low living standards of 80 percent of the population. Nikolai Kurilovich (Liberal Democratic Party of Russia) said that the state should take better care of children from divorced families and pay them alimonies. And Nina Ostakina (Communist

Party) pointed out that during the time Zurabov had taken to present his report, 340 people had died in Russia.

"*Since 1986 Russia's life expectancy has been declining and at least 30 percent of this decline can be accounted for by environmental causes.*"

Environmental Pollution Is a Major Problem in Russia

Mark A. Smith

In the following viewpoint, Mark A. Smith argues that the environmental situation in Russia is dire. Air and water pollution, contamination of the soil by heavy metals from industrial activity, nuclear and chemical munitions waste, and radioactive contamination are so severe that, given the lack of effective environmental controls, the usual remediation is to fence off and abandon affected areas. In heavily populated areas where this is not possible, Smith says, the incidence of birth defects, respiratory and other environment-related illnesses, and early death continues to rise. Mark A. Smith is a senior lecturer at the Conflict Studies Research Centre, a college of the Defence Academy of the United Kingdom that analyzes potential causes of conflict in Central Asia and the Baltic states, and the author of numerous studies of Russian geopolitical issues.

As you read, consider the following questions:

1. How many Russians breathe air and drink water that fails to meet required standards, according to Smith?

2. What are the sources and quantities of toxic waste dumped into the Caspian Sea each year, according to the author?

3. Why does the author consider legislation that permits Russia to become a large-scale importer and processor of spent nuclear fuel a dangerous development?

The Soviet Union bequeathed the Russian Federation an unenviable environmental and ecological legacy. The emphasis that the Soviet system had placed on heavy industry, largely for the purposes of national security, meant that environmental concerns took second place to the need for industrial development. Little concern was expressed during the Soviet period over environmental issues, although it would be wrong to say that there was complete silence. Voices were raised during the 1960s, for example, over pollution in [Siberian] Lake Baikal. By and large, however, green issues were not discussed. . . .

The contraction experienced by the Russian economy in the immediate post-communist years meant that there was a reduction in pollution levels due to the decline in industrial output. However the fundamental problems remained, and the ability of the Russian state to clean up existing environmental problems and to provide environmental protection to a degree comparable with that of western industrialised countries was, to say the least, extremely limited. The following points give an overview of the environmental situation in the Russian Federation since 1991.

It is reckoned that one child in three may be ill because of environmental pollution. A 1996 joint US-Russian government study found that one-quarter of kindergarten pupils in one city had lead concentrations above the threshold at which intelligence is impaired, while a US government study noted a rise in the incidence of waterborne diseases and environmentally related birth defects. A Russian government report cited air pollution as a contributing factor to 17 percent of childhood and 10 percent of adult illnesses.

Through the 1990s, nearly 100 million Russian citizens in 200 large cities were estimated to be breathing air with pollution levels that exceeded Russian ambient air quality standards, and most of the country's rivers and lakes were classified as "moderately polluted" or "polluted".

Data from the late 1990s indicate that more than 90 cities had annual concentrations of particulate matter and nitrogen dioxide that exceeded WHO [World Health Organization] standards. The worst areas are the cities of Moscow, Chelyabinsk, Norilsk in northern Siberia, and Kemerovo in southern Siberia.

About one-half of Russia's population consumes drinking water that fails to meet required standards. In St. Petersburg, according to official reports, a litre of drinking water contains about 20 micrograms of chlorinated hydrocarbons, twice the level permitted under German standards. In Kemerovo, there is 320 times the German limit on chloroform in drinking water. Seven out of 10 children born there come into the world sick. It has been estimated that the cost of raising the quality of Russia's drinking water supply to official standards could be as high as $200 billion.

Heavy metals, hydrocarbons and organic chemicals from industrial activity contaminated more than 2 million hectares of soil [a hectare is 10,000 square meters] and industrial activity in many cities has probably contributed to a high rate of respiratory diseases and a high incidence of lead-related childhood mental development problems.

Since 1986 Russia's life expectancy has been declining and at least 30 percent of this decline can be accounted for by environmental causes. Specialists estimate that 350,000 early deaths occur annually. The average male life expectancy is about 59 years. ·

Nuclear waste and chemical munitions contamination is so extensive and costly to reverse that remedial efforts are likely to continue to be limited largely to fencing off affected areas.

The number of vehicles on the road has increased rapidly since 1991, and their emissions offset reductions in industrial air pollution caused by reduced economic activity and greater reliance on natural gas. Leaded petrol [gasoline] is still widely used. Solid waste generation has increased substantially due to adoption of Western-style consumption patterns. Russian municipalities, however, lack management expertise and landfill capacity to cope with disposal problems.

Hazardous waste disposal problems are extensive and growing. Russian officials estimate that about 200 tonnes [metric tons] of the most highly toxic and hazardous wastes are dumped illegally each year in locations that lack effective environmental or public health protections or oversight.

Radioactive contamination caused by nuclear powered submarines and ships of both the Northern Fleet and Pacific Fleet has become a major problem. Reporting on this has raised issues of civil rights including the right to freedom of information.

A team of Russian experts has pegged overall economic losses from environmental degradation at 10 to 12 percent of GDP [gross domestic product]. By contrast the loss in western industrialised countries is around 1 to 2 percent of GDP.

Spending on Cleanup Is Dropping

Budgetary constraints have made cleaning up the environment much more problematical. Spending on the environment is less than 0.5 percent of total federal budget spending—a significant drop from the modest levels of the late Soviet period.

In the 2005 federal budget, spending on the environment amounted to 0.15 percent of the total budget. In 2006, the figure was slightly less. In 1999, federal budget allocations to the principal environmental protection agency in Russia were less than one-quarter of the amount requested. By contrast, in the 1970s Japan had to spend 5 percent of the country's budget to overcome what were her then-disastrous environmental problems.

Spending on maintaining drinking water quality in Russia, for example, is down 90 percent from the levels of the 1980s. The monitoring of the environment has also suffered from funding shortfalls. Although the size of the observational network for water quality was roughly the same in 2000 as at the end of the Soviet era 10 years earlier, the quality of the data declined due to inadequate staff training, obsolete equipment, irregular maintenance, and poor data quality assurance procedures. In 1998, fewer than 40 percent of the laboratories that analyzed water quality were certified. Furthermore, the infrastructure of municipal drinking water and wastewater treatment facilities—which was funded predominantly by central budgets in the Soviet era—has deteriorated due to deferred maintenance and insufficient capital investment by local municipalities. These issues probably contributed to significant reported increases in gastroenteritis, hepatitis A and bacterial dysentery in the 1990s.

The Baltic Sea

Untreated sewage from St. Petersburg is a major source of Baltic pollution. In June 2003, Sweden's Commission on Marine Environment warned that the Baltic Sea was in a "critical" condition and in danger of dying unless pollution from St. Petersburg is drastically cut [St. Petersburg and Sweden are on the Baltic Sea]. Untreated sewage flows straight into the Neva river, and from there to the Baltic. In 2003, Alexander Ridko, then head of the health and ecology commission at the

St. Petersburg legislative assembly, said that only 60 per cent of the water dumped into the sea from St. Petersburg has been filtered sufficiently. Half of the fish species in the Baltic are at levels below the critical biological level, while pregnant Swedish women have been warned not to eat herring—a diet staple—because of dioxins. Massive over-fishing in the Baltic has decimated stocks, and pollution has meant they are unable to grow again.

In 2003 it was announced that the European Bank for Reconstruction and Development (EBRD) was lending 35.4 million euros to complete the construction of the St. Petersburg Southwest Waste Water Treatment Plant (SWWTP). Construction began in the Soviet era but was halted after 1991 because of shortage of funds. Two key related projects [are] construction of inlets to collect the sewage for treatment (€15 million) and the SWWTP's separate sludge incinerator (€22 million).

The Caspian Sea

This is a problem which Russia shares with the other states [bordering the Caspian Sea]. The dumping of waste products into the Caspian by inflowing rivers is a major problem. About 130 rivers flow into the Caspian. About 80 percent of the water comes from the Russian River Volga. Untreated waste from the Volga—into which half the population of Russia and most of its heavy industry drains its sewage—empties directly into the Caspian Sea, while pesticides and chemicals from agricultural run-off are threats to the sea's flora and fauna. Scientists estimate that each year an average of 60,000 tonnes of petroleum byproducts, 24,000 tonnes of sulfites, 400,000 tonnes of chlorine and 25,000 tonnes of chlorine are dumped into the sea. Concentrations of oil and phenols in the northern sea are four to six times higher than the maximum recommended standards. Around Baku in Azerbaijan, where oil drilling and industrialization have been happening for almost a century, these pollutants are ten to sixteen times higher.

Hazards in and around the Caspian

Aktobe

DON-VOLGA CANAL
Volga
KAPUSTIN YAR
Vologad
AZGYR

KAZAKHSTAN

TUHLAYA BALKA
SEDIMENTATION TANK
Atyrau

Elista
Astrakhan

RUSSIA

Stavropol

TENGIZ
OIL FIELD

ARAL
SEA

Groznyl
Vladikavkaz

Bautino

CASPIAN
SEA
Aktau
Makhachkala

MINING SITE
KOSHKAR-ATA
TAILING POND
MAEK ATOMNY
KOMBINAT
WASTE SITE

SAY UTES

UZBEKISTAN

UZEN
OIL FIELD

Tskhinvali

Derbent

GEORGIA Tbilisi

ARMENIA
Yerevan

Sumgait

MERCURY
WASTE SITE

KARA
BOGAZ
GOL

NAKHICHEVAN
(AZER.)
Nakhichevan

Baku
Dubendi

TURKMENISTAN

Turkmen bashi RADIOACTIVE WASTE

Araks

Tabriz

Balkanabat
Khazar

Gyzyl-Arbat

KARA-KUM CANAL

IODINE AND
BROMINE PLANT

Ashkabad

IRAN

Rasht

Gasan
Kuli
Ramsar Babol

Bender

Gorgan

IRAN

IRAQ

Qazvin

Sari

Tehran

0   200   400 km

Legend

◯ Oil and gas drilling

‐ ‐ ‐ Projected off-shore pipelines

▦ Oil wells flooded and leaking

▦ Area under exploration for oil and gas (high potential)

▦ Polluted sea (oil, pesticides, chemicals, heavy metals or bacteriological origin)

▦ Polluted soils and land degradation

⬚ Soil salinisation

═══ Polluted rivers (industry and municipal sewage water)

⟊→ Land-base source of river pollution (mainly heavy industries)

⊠ Identified poorly stored hazardous industrial waste site or polluting industrial activities

⊼ Former nuclear testing site

➜ Main direction of sand-dust storm causing salt transfers toward arable lands of the Volga region

Thousands of seals in the Caspian Sea have died since 2000 due to pollution that weakened their immune systems, and overfishing, especially of sturgeon, has caused a dramatic decline in fish stocks. In the 1980s the average annual catch of sturgeon was approximately 25,000 tonnes of sturgeon, by 1994 the legal catch stood at 7,000 tonnes. Poaching is rife.

Mineral deposit exploitation, particularly oil and gas extraction and pipeline construction, have contributed to the pollution of about 30,000 hectares of land. In August 2001, Tengizchevroil, the ChevronTexaco-led international consortium developing the giant Tengiz oil field in western Kazakhstan, was fined around $75 million for ecological damage. In addition, Kazakhstan forced Agip KCO, the consortium developing the offshore Kashagan field in shallow water, to halt operations temporarily and pay a hefty fine after several oil spills from exploratory wells operated by the consortium. The inability of the [Caspian-bordering] states to reach agreement on the legal status of the Caspian Sea makes environmental control and cooperation more difficult.

However there have been several initiatives to boost regional cooperation in protecting the environment, including the establishment of the Caspian Environment Programme (CEP) in conjunction with the World Bank's Global Environmental Facility. The aim of the CEP is defined as "environmentally sustainable development and management of the Caspian environment, including living resources and water quality, so as to obtain the utmost long-term benefits for the human populations of the region, while protecting human health, ecological integrity, and the region's sustainability for future generations."

Far East

In addition to the problems caused by the Pacific Fleet [one of Russia's four naval fleets], major problems were caused in the Russian Far East in 2004 when the Amur river was heavily polluted by a leakage from a benzene [a highly toxic carcinogen, used as an industrial solvent] factory belonging to Petro-China upstream in northeast China. As a result allowable levels of concentration for different types of phenol [benzene breaks down into phenols] were exceeded. The chlorophenol group now actively exceeds the allowable level of concentration by almost 30 times.

Lead poisoning is a serious problem in [southeastern Russian region] Primorsky Krai and the rest of Russian Far East. There is little control of industrial pollution. Many industries use old equipment and old technologies that increase environmental contamination. At the same time there are very few government regulations regarding the risk of lead poisoning and few studies addressing the relationship between lead contamination of the environment and the health of the population. Some children that were tested in Vladivostok, Spassk, Kavalerovo, and Dalnegorsk had blood lead concentrations over 80 g/dl [micrograms per decilitre]. The present Russian "safe" standard is 8 g/dl. . . .

Nuclear Waste Processing

In 2001 [then-president] Vladimir Putin signed into a law a package of legislation that would permit Russia to become a large scale importer and processor of spent nuclear fuel. Russia could import around 20,000 tonnes of foreign spent nuclear fuel in the next 20 years and earn around $20 billion on such operations. Around $7 billion of the earnings is to be spent on various environmental and social programmes. Russia currently has about 15,000 tonnes of her own nuclear waste. There is one processing plant, Mayak (RT-1), near Chelyabinsk in the southern [Ural Mountains]. It is old, and is not capable of processing the nuclear waste it currently receives.

The level of radioactive contamination in the area around Mayak is extremely high. Lake Karachay, adjacent to the Mayak complex, is now considered to be one of the most polluted spots on Earth. It has been reported to contain 120 million curies of radioactive waste, including seven times the amount of strontium-90 and cesium-137 that was released in the April 1986 explosion at the Chernobyl nuclear power plant in Ukraine [the worst nuclear power plant accident in history].

The construction of another plant at Krasnoyarsk (RT-2) started in 1976, but was not completed due to lack of funds. In 1985, a storage pool for waste from VVER-1000 reactors, which was to be a part of RT-2, was commissioned. The rest of the construction was frozen in 1989. Later the initial design was drastically modified. The entire plant will now be commissioned not earlier than 2015. The storage pool has a capacity of 6,000 tonnes and is more than 50 percent full. The pool requires overhaul and repairs.

Minatom [Ministry for Atomic Energy] does not plan immediate reprocessing of nuclear waste, and plans to dry-store the fuel for around 40 to 50 years. Moreover the power of Gosatomnadzor, the nuclear regulatory authority, is limited. The government is partial towards Minatom, as it sees the development of nuclear power as a higher priority than environmental protection.

Nuclear Submarine Contamination

This has been an extremely controversial issue nationally and internationally, due to the whistleblowing activities of former military personnel, and has raised issues of press freedom, human rights and state security. . . .

The infrastructure of the Pacific Fleet is dilapidated and perhaps the most difficult naval nuclear dismantlement project in Russia. The Northern Fleet now has a well-established infrastructure, but the Pacific Fleet, which is home to some 40 submarines awaiting dismantlement with their nuclear fuel on board, poses a bigger challenge. These rusted-out derelict subs are moored from 100 to 1,000 kilometres from the nearest dismantlement point. In all, some 14,000 fuel assemblies remain on board. The amount stored on technical service vessels (i.e vessels that service nuclear submarines) is unknown.

The lack of maintenance of submarines has long been a major problem. A reactor explosion occurred at Chazma Bay in 1985 during refuelling. Another sub off Kamchatka sank in 1997 due to its rust-ridden state. The poor state of the Pacific Fleet's submarines make further accidents likely. The radioisotope thermoelectric generators (RTGs) that dot the eastern coast are also unguarded health hazards that have been used in the past to power navigation beacons, but are now dilapidated and neglected.

The Pacific Fleet has two storage sites for radioactive waste—one on Kamchatka and the other on the Shkotovo Peninsula, southeast of Vladivostok. Spent nuclear fuel (SNF) is stored at Shkotovo, which suffered an accident in 1980. There is, as yet, no publicly available data on how much is stored by the Pacific Fleet. The SNF is transported to Mayak in the southern Urals, but there is no direct rail-head, meaning the waste is transported over 60 kilometres of bumpy roads for rail shipment. Spills of waste have been recorded.

The willingness of the Russian authorities to prosecute whistleblowers under state secrecy laws, and to accuse them of acting for foreign intelligence services is obviously aimed at deterring journalists and environmental activists from investigating cases of pollution at military installations, which makes it difficult for the public to become fully aware of the extent of the problem. The armed forces do have an administration dealing with ecological security, which was formed in July 1992. However the impact of its work is limited.

Several foreign countries, most notably Norway and Japan, have played a major role in programmes to dismantle obsolete Russian nuclear submarines in an environmentally safe fashion. Situated near major Russian naval bases, they have an obvious interest in reducing the environmental threat posed by these submarines. Although these programmes have yielded positive results, the regions where the Pacific and Northern Fleets are based are still subject to a high degree of radioactive contamination.

State Policy Toward the Environment

During the Soviet period, minimal concern was shown for the environment. It was only in 1988 that a Union Committee for Environmental Protection was formed. The Union Committee's charge included the regulation and enforcement of environmental standards, management of "nature protection", and the coordination of environmental activities of the various ministries and agencies. The Union Committee for Environmental Protection became the Russian Federation's State Committee for Environmental Protection (Goskomekologiya) in 1991. . . .

In May 2000, President Vladimir Putin eliminated Goskomekologiya altogether and placed its responsibilities and personnel in the Federation's Ministry of Natural Resources.

Putin's decision to abolish Goskomekologiya signified a downgrading of concern for the environment by the state. Goskomekologiya was concerned with enforcing and monitoring environmental standards, rules and regulations. However by merging Goskomekoloigya with the Ministry of Natural Resources, its capacity to control environmental pollution was constrained. The Ministry is primarily concerned with the exploitation of natural resources for economic growth and development, rather than conservation which may constrain economic growth.

In addition to the merging of Goskomekologiya with the Ministry of Natural Resources, there have been several other negative trends from the standpoint of environmental protection since 1995.

- The State Atomic Inspectorate has lost much of its mandate;

- The State Sanitary and Epidemic Inspectorate was demoted to a department within the Ministry of Health;

- The Department of Environmental Protection and the Use of Natural Resources within the Presidential Administration has been formally abolished;

- The Security Council Interagency Commission on Ecological Security has virtually no power or influence;

- The Governmental Commission on Resolving the Problem of Radioactive Waste has been formally abolished.

In November 2001 the Russian Ministry of Natural Resources issued an ecological policy doctrine, which put forward a 10 year plan for cleaning up the Russian environment. However little has been done to ensure that this plan will be realised. A new law on the environment came into force in 2002, but this has done little to improve the situation. The emphasis on economic growth is the main reason why the legislative programmes for protecting the environment have had little impact.

> "When oil revenues flood a nation with
> a fragile system of democratic checks
> and balances, dysfunctional politics and
> economics ensue."

Russia's Reliance on Oil Exports May Lead to Its Downfall

Moisés Naím

In the following viewpoint, Moisés Naím warns that a rich "petro-state," such as Russia, without strong democratic institutions and independent regulatory agencies to administer its oil-based economy will fall into "poverty, inequality, and corruption." The author is former minister of trade and industry of Venezuela, which, he believes, is a similarly troubled oil-rich but politically unstable state. Naím is editor-in-chief of Foreign Policy, *a magazine of global politics and economics published by the Carnegie Endowment for International Peace in Washington, D.C., and the author of eight books, including* Illicit: How Smugglers, Traffickers, and Copycats Are Hijacking the Global Economy.

Moisés Naím, "Russia's Oily Future," *Foreign Policy,* January/February 2004. Copyright © 2008 *Foreign Policy.* All rights reserved. Reproduced by permission.

As you read, consider the following questions:

1. What percentage of Russia's economy, export earnings, and total tax revenues is accounted for by oil and gas, according to Naím?

2. How does an oil-based economy hinder the growth of Russian agriculture, manufacturing, and tourism, in Naím's view?

3. Why is an economy dominated by oil bad for Russians whether the oil industry is privatized or state-owned, according to the author?

Russia's future will be defined as much by the geology of its subsoil as by the ideology of its leaders. Unfortunately, whereas policymakers can choose their ideology, they don't have much leeway when it comes to geology. Russia has a lot of oil, and this inescapable geological fact will determine many of the policy choices available to its leaders. Oil and gas now account for roughly 20 percent of Russia's economy, 55 percent of its export earnings, and 40 percent of its total tax revenues. Russia is the world's second largest oil exporter after Saudi Arabia, and its subsoil contains 33 percent of the world's gas reserves. It already supplies 30 percent of Europe's gas needs. In the future, Russia's oil and gas industry will become even more important, as no other sector can be as internationally competitive, grow as rapidly, or be as profitable. Thus, Russia risks becoming, and in many respects may already be, a "petro-state." The arrest of oil magnate Mikhail Khodorkovsky sparked a debate over what kind of country Russia will be.[1] In this discussion, Russia's characteristics as a petro-state deserve as much attention as its factional struggles.

1. Khodorkovsky became the richest man in Russia through financial deals that favored a small group of insiders when Russia privatized its economy. He developed political ambitions and criticized the Kremlin, however. Western media suggest his arrest on tax evasion charges (and 10-year jail sentence) was politically motivated.

Russia Can Barely Meet Its Own Growing Demand for Natural Gas

Gazprom, the Russian natural-gas giant, is often portrayed as the 1,000-pound gorilla of the energy world. . . .

The surprising Achilles' heel of Gazprom is that it produces only about 550 billion cubic meters (bcm) of gas—just enough to supply its own domestic market. It relies on cheap imports from Central Asia to meet the majority of its other commitments to customers in Europe. . . .

Gazprom hasn't opened up a new gas field since 1991, and its existing fields are dwindling. A recent report by the Russian Industry and Energy Ministry warned that if the decline continued, Russia may be unable to service even its own domestic gas needs by 2010, and recommended doubling prices, a conservation move that has upset business and could also put a damper on economic growth.

Owen Matthews, "Russia's Big Energy Secret,"
Newsweek, *December 22, 2007.*

Petro-States: Lots of Oil, Not Much Prosperity

Petro-states are oil-rich countries plagued by weak institutions, a poorly functioning public sector, and a high concentration of power and wealth. Their population is chronically frustrated by the lack of proportion between their nation's oil wealth and their widespread poverty. Nigeria and Venezuela are good examples.

That Russia has lots of oil is old news. What's new is the dramatically enhanced role that changes in Russian politics, oil technology, and energy markets have given to its petroleum sector. Throughout the 1990s, privatization in Russia and innovations in exploration and drilling technologies brought into production oil fields that had hitherto been underperforming or completely off-limits. To energy companies worried about growing domestic instability among the major oil exporters of the Middle East, Russia became an even more attractive hedge. Regardless of its political turmoil, Russia will continue to appeal to oil companies, which know how to operate profitably in countries with weak property rights and unstable politics. Thus, while the Khodorkovsky affair may temporarily scare away some investors, Russia's beguiling geology will eventually attract energy companies that cannot afford to be left out of some of the world's richest oil reservoirs.

But when oil revenues flood a nation with a fragile system of democratic checks and balances, dysfunctional politics and economics ensue, and a petro-state emerges. A strong democracy and an effective public sector explain why oil has not distorted the United States or Norway as it has Nigeria and Venezuela. A lot of oil combined with weak public institutions produces poverty, inequality, and corruption. It also undermines democracy. No petro-state has succeeded in converting oil into prosperity for the majority of the population.

An Oil Economy Doesn't Create Jobs

An economy that relies mostly on oil exports inevitably ends up with an exchange rate that makes imported goods less expensive and exports more costly. This overvalued exchange rate makes other sectors—agriculture, manufacturing, tourism—less internationally competitive and hinders their growth. Petro-states also have jobless, volatile economic growth. Oil generates export revenues and taxes for the state, but it creates few jobs. Despite its economic heft, Russia's oil and gas industry employs only around 2 million workers out of a total workforce of 67 million. Also, because the international price of oil is volatile, petro-states suffer constant and debilitating economic boom-bust cycles. The busts lead to banking crises and public budget cuts that hurt the poor who critically depend on government programs. Russia already experienced this effect in 1998 when the drop in oil prices sparked a financial crash. If oil prices fall [sharply], Russia will surely face another bout of painful economic instability.

Petro-states also suffer from a narrow tax base, with the bulk of government revenues coming from just a few large taxpayers. In Russia, the 10 largest companies account for more than half of total tax revenues. Weak governmental accountability is a typical side effect of this dependency, as the link between the electorate and government spending is indirect and tenuous.

An Oil Economy Does Promote Corruption

The political consequences are also corrosive. Thanks to the inevitable concentration of the oil industry into a few large firms, owners and managers acquire enormous political clout. In turn, corruption often thrives, as a handful of politicians and government regulators make decisions that are worth millions to these companies. Nationalizing the oil industry fails to solve these problems: State-owned oil companies quickly become relatively independent political actors that are rife with corruption, inefficiency, and politicization, and can dominate other weak public institutions. Privatizing the industry without strong and independent regulatory and tax agencies is also not a solution, as unbridled private monopolists can be as predatory as public ones.

In petro-states, bitter fights over the control and distribution of the nation's oil rents become the gravitational center of political life. It is no accident that the current crisis in Russia hinges on control of the country's largest oil company and the political uses of its profits.

But Russia is not Nigeria and has yet to become a full-fledged petro-state. It is a large, complex country with a highly educated population, a relatively strong technological base, and a still somewhat diversified economy. A strong democracy could help Russia compensate for the economic and political weaknesses that plague all countries dominated by oil. Russia is still struggling to overcome the crippling effects of its ideological past. Let's hope it will also be able to avoid the crippling effects of its geological present.

| *"Moscow has become an impediment . . .*
to the fight against Islamic terror."

Russia's Relationship with the Middle East Is Perilous

Igor Khrestin and John Elliott

In the following viewpoint, Igor Khrestin and John Elliott accuse Russia of pursuing a risky strategy in the war on terror. Officially a partner of the United States in the war on terror, Russia really only fights a domestic war on radical Islamism, in its Chechnya province, where its territorial security is at stake. Meanwhile, as the authors explain, Russia has become a patron of the Organisation of the Islamic Conference, makes nuclear and arms deals with Middle Eastern rogue states, and invites the representatives of terrorist groups like Hamas to Moscow. Khrestin and Elliott call this a calculated strategy to advance Russia's position in the Middle East at the expense of the United States and buy immunity from Muslim-world criticism of its violent crackdown in Chechnya. The authors further argue that this strategy is destabilizing the Middle East, and Islamic terrorists will attack Russia anyway. Igor Khrestin is a research assistant in Russian studies at the American Enterprise Institute, a conserva-

Igor Khrestin and John Elliott, "Russia and the Middle East," *Middle East Quarterly,* vol. xiv, Winter 2007. Copyright © 2007 The Middle East Forum. Reproduced by permission.

tive think tank in Washington, D.C. John Elliott is a research associate at the Council on Foreign Relations, a nonpartisan New York-based organization that promotes debate on foreign policy issues and understanding of U.S. interests in the world.

As you read, consider the following questions:

1. What did both parties hope to gain when Russia was granted observer status by the Organisation of the Islamic Conference, according to the authors?

2. How has Russia supported Iran's nuclear program, despite awareness that its aims are military as well as civilian, according to the authors?

3. What contradictions do the authors find in Russia's relations with Israel?

Where does Moscow stand in the fight against Islamism and the global war against terror? Facing the Chechen threat at home, the Russian government might be sympathetic to U.S. and even Israeli concerns. Not so. Despite U.S. declarations that Washington and Moscow were "increasingly united by common values" and that Russia was "a partner in the war on terror," examination of Russian president Vladimir Putin's policy toward the Middle East suggests that Moscow has become an impediment both to the fight against Islamist terror and Washington's desire to promote democracy in the Middle East. The 2006 U.S. National Security Strategy [a White House document] reinforces that U.S. policymakers should not only "encourage Russia to respect the values of freedom and democracy at home" but also cease "imped[ing] the cause of freedom and democracy" in regions vital to the war on terror. While Russian officials denounce U.S. criticism, the Kremlin's coddling of Iranian hard-liners, its reaction to the "cartoon jihad," its invitation to Hamas to Moscow, and its flawed Chechen policy all cast doubt on Moscow's motivations.

While President Bill Clinton had focused his Middle East policy on Israeli-Palestinian peace talks, his strategy toward the broader Middle East was more detached. He was content to pursue dual containment toward Iraq and Iran and follow a status quo policy toward North Africa and the Arabian Peninsula. The 9-11 terrorist attacks focused U.S. foreign policy on the Middle East. President George W. Bush asserted that the region "must be a focus of American policy for decades to come" and declared a "forward strategy of freedom in the Middle East." Putin, too, made the Middle East an area of increasing focus. But in contrast to his rhetoric of cooperation—he was the first foreign leader to call Bush on 9-11—he has pursued a contradictory strategy to bolster Russian influence at U.S. expense.

The Chechen Lens

Nothing shapes Putin's thinking about terrorism and the Middle East more than Chechnya [a province engaged in a war for independence since the breakup of the Soviet Union]. While Islamist terrorism threatens U.S. security, the Chechen conflict threatens both Russian security and its territorial integrity. The conflict in Russia's Chechnya province has claimed over one hundred thousand lives since President Boris Yeltsin ordered the Russian military into Chechnya in 1994. After the 1996 cease-fire, Chechnya dissolved into anarchy, becoming the "Somalia of the Caucasus." Foreign jihadists infiltrated the Chechen leadership. In 1999, Vladimir Putin, newly-appointed prime minister, ordered Russian troops to reassert order. His tough stance catapulted him into political prominence and, eventually, the presidency.

Putin and Bush initially cooperated in the war against the Taliban [Afghanistan's Islamic fundamentalists]. The Russian leader complied with U.S. requests to build bases in [nearby] Uzbekistan and Kyrgyzstan for use in the war against the Afghan Islamists. In April 2002, U.S. and Russian militaries cooperated to dislodge terror groups from Georgia's Pankisi Gorge. The following month, the two leaders declared, "We are partners, and we will cooperate to advance stability, security, and economic integration, and to jointly counter global challenges and to help resolve regional conflicts."

Putin's domestic war on terrorism enjoyed only limited success. Russian security forces did impose some order in Chechnya, but the Kremlin was unable to stem Chechen and Islamist terrorism on Russian soil. In 2002, 120 died in a rescue attempt after Chechen rebels took 800 people hostage in a Moscow theater. Two years later, several hundred children died after terrorists seized a school in Beslan. Even after the subsequent crackdown, Russian forces have not been able to stop Chechen Islamist raids into neighboring provinces as they seek to build an "Islamic Republic of the North Caucasus." Terrorists continue to take advantage of endemic Russian corruption. An independent Russian daily observed that "a police officer or soldier is killed in the Caucasus practically every day;" a senior military official admitted that the situation in Chechnya is "far from ideal."

Faced with only marginal gains at home, Putin changed tack. Rather than continue cooperation with Washington on the broader war on terror, he sought to cut a deal. In 2003, he asked to join the Organisation of the Islamic Conference (OIC) [an affiliation of Muslim states promoting Islamic solidarity], even though with only 20 million Muslims—about 15 percent of the population—Russia lacked the required 50 percent minimum Muslim population. While the OIC did not grant Russia full membership, it did grant Moscow observer status. The relationship was symbiotic: the OIC saw Moscow as a patron that could offset U.S. pressure while Moscow received de facto immunity from criticism of Russian policy in Chechnya as a result of OIC reluctance to interfere in the internal affairs of member-states, even honorary ones. Putin further outlined his vision of alliance with the Islamic world when, addressing the newly-elected Chechen parliament in December 2005, Putin called Russia "a faithful, reliable, and

© Mike Mosedale CartoonStock.com

dedicated promoter ... of the interests of the Islamic world" and "its best and most reliable partner and friend."

Arming Iran

The desire both to cut a deal and stymie Washington also explains Moscow's policy toward Tehran [capital of Iran]. Russian and Iranian interests are historically divergent. The two countries fought intermittently throughout the nineteenth century, and Soviet leaders supported separatist movements in Iran in the twentieth century. Their perceived spheres of influence overlap in the Caucasus and the Caspian. The 1979 Islamic Revolution may have torn Iran away from alliance with the United States, but it did not bring Tehran and Moscow any closer. Revolutionary leader Ayatollah Ruhollah Khomeini considered the Soviet Union to be "godless" and purged leftists from the revolutionary coalition.

But a February 1989 visit by Soviet foreign minister Eduard Shevardnadze and a reciprocal visit to Moscow by then-[Iran parliament] speaker Ali Akbar Hashemi Rafsanjani four months later cemented a détente [truce]. Relations expanded with Moscow after the Soviet Union's collapse. On August 25, 1992, Tehran and Moscow signed an US$800 million deal for Russian companies to build two nuclear reactors at Bushehr [Iran]. While this contract predates Putin's presidency, the Russian leader turned a blind eye to signs that the Iranian program was not entirely civilian. Five years after Rafsanjani threatened to use nuclear weapons against Israel, and despite an International Atomic Energy Agency finding that Iran was in noncompliance with the nuclear nonproliferation treaty's safeguards agreement, Russian foreign minister Sergei Lavrov insists that the Iranian program "is conducted fully in accordance with international norms."

So what explains Russian behavior? Maintaining nuclear trade with Tehran enabled Putin to cement a tacit agreement in which Iran declines to interfere in Chechnya and other Islamist causes which threaten Russia. Winning Iranian acquiescence is especially important given its proximity to Russia's troubled south. In exchange, the Kremlin shields the Iranian government from Western pressure. Russian unwillingness to accept sanctions against Iran for its nuclear noncompliance has vexed Washington, as has Moscow's refusal to force an Iranian reaction to the May 2006 European Union and U.S. package of incentives.

Any Middle Eastern government which seeks Moscow's support understands it must either side with the Russian struggle against Chechen separatists or, at a minimum, agree not to meddle. With the end of the Cold War, the Israeli government has sought to better its relations with Moscow. Since 1999, Israeli intelligence has shared information with their Russian counterparts and has assisted Russian forces in training and border security. Israeli officials have likened the Chechen separatists to Palestinian terrorists. Damascus [capital of Syria], too, has assisted Russia diplomatically. In September 2005, Syrian president Bashar al-Assad welcomed the pro-Moscow president of Chechnya, Alu Alkhanov, to Damascus, granting the embattled Chechen leader some international legitimacy.

The commercial factor is also a bonus. The Russian government has secured lucrative contracts with several states that Washington considers pariahs. In December 2005, the Iranian government signed a billion dollar arms deal that included twenty-nine Tor M1 missile defense systems to protect the Bushehr nuclear facility. The Russian government has also sold Strelets missiles to Syria. Putin halted sales of even more sophisticated weaponry only after vigorous U.S. and Israeli protest. That Iran is also oil-rich is added incentive; Russia has $750 million invested in energy projects there. The Russian oil firm Lukoil seeks to move 23 percent of production to the Middle East by 2015.

Russia's Cartoon Jihad

Bush characterizes the U.S. fight as a "war with Islamic fascists." Putin, too, has cracked down on Islamist terror in Russia. But what works at home is not necessarily what Putin embraces for those outside Russia. On February 4, 2006, protests erupted in many Muslim countries against cartoons depicting the Prophet Muhammad, which had been published months before in the Danish daily *Jyllands-Posten*. In Lebanon and Syria, mobs sacked the Danish embassy and, in Libya, they attacked an Italian consulate. But rather than stand up for free speech—as did many outside the Middle East—the Russian government sided with the Islamists.

Konstantin Kosachev, chairman of the Duma's (parliament) International Affairs Committee, chided the Danish government for allowing such cartoons to be published. "The [Danish] prime minister washed his hands of the whole matter, with the usual comments, chapter and verse, about freedom of speech," Kosachev said, before chiding the Danes for citing the right of free speech as reason not to crack down on "anti-

Russian hysteria over Chechnya in Denmark" a few years earlier. Then, three days after the mass protests erupted, Putin said, "One should reflect 100 times before publishing or drawing something. . . . If a state cannot prevent such publications, it should at least ask for forgiveness."

To drive home the point, on February 17, Andrei Dorinin, acting mayor of the southern Russian city of Volgograd, shut down the local paper *Gorodskie Vesti*, after it printed a cartoon depicting the Prophet Muhammad along with Jesus, Moses, and Buddha. The government also charged Anna Smirnova, editor of *Nash Region* in Vologda, with "inciting racial hatred"—an offense punishable by up to five years in prison, according to article 282 of the Russian criminal code—after her paper republished the original *Jyllands-Posten* cartoons. She was fined 100,000 rubles (about US$3,700). The paper's owners, citing concerns over the "safety of the journalists," shut down the newspaper.

What makes the Russian government's actions curious is that they initiated the crackdown absent any significant public outcry, let alone riots, against the cartoons. According to a nationwide poll conducted by the Levada Center, only 14 percent of respondents were "outraged" by the Prophet Muhammad cartoons; the plurality simply did not care. The reactions of Russia's religious leaders were likewise muted. Mufti Talgat Tadzhuddin, head of the Central Muslim Spiritual Directorate, noted that "in a cultured society, it is necessary that there be cultured people."

While local politics played a part in the crackdowns, the general Kremlin reaction showed that the fight against Islamism was relative. While Putin will neither tolerate terrorism nor the ideology behind it at home, he will at times justify that same extremism abroad if it wins Moscow points in the Islamic world, prolongs the tacit agreement against Islamic countries' interference in Chechnya, and undercuts the general U.S. and European diplomatic position in the Middle East.

Andrei Serenko, an expert at the Fund for Development for Information Policy, explained, "To prove Vladimir Putin's thesis that 'a strong Russia is a defender of Muslims,' [the Kremlin] can sacrifice a regional newspaper."

Hamas Tours Moscow

Perhaps nothing underlined the relativity of Moscow's fight against terror as much as the Kremlin's 2006 invitation to Moscow of a Hamas delegation.[1] In February 2006, Putin announced, "We are willing in the near future to invite the authorities of Hamas to Moscow to carry out talks." The State Department reacted cautiously. Spokesman Sean McCormack warned that ". . . we would certainly expect that Russia would deliver that same message" to Hamas, namely to renounce violence, recognize Israel, and respect previous Palestinian and international agreements.

While Moscow had long supported the Palestine Liberation Organization and lobbied for the creation of the Palestinian state, Putin's outreach to Hamas broke with tradition. Mikhail Margelov, the chairman of the international relations committee of the Federation Council, Russia's upper house [of parliament], had praised the Israeli assassination of Hamas spiritual leader Sheikh Ahmad Yasin. When a Hamas suicide bomber killed seventeen people in Beersheba in August 2004, the Russian Foreign Ministry issued a statement condemning "the new barbarous foray by the extremists," and declaring, "We are convinced that no political or other purposes can be reached by means of violence and terror."

Hamas leaders seized the opportunity proffered by Putin. Hamas spokesman Sami Abu Zuhri said, "We salute the Russian position and . . . accept it with the aim of strengthening our relations with the West and particularly with the Russian

1. Hamas is one of the chief Palestinian organizations and has both military and political arms. Its political arm won the Palestinian Authority's legislative elections in January 2006.

government." The Hamas delegation met with Lavrov, toured the capital with the leaders of Russia's Muslim community, and had an audience with the patriarch of the Russian Orthodox Church. The Russian government's engagement with Hamas did not lead the group to abandon terrorism. One Russian journalist concluded, "Moscow invited the Palestinians just to invite them, and Hamas came just to come."

The Russian press was less forgiving than the Kremlin. In the press conference, an *Izvestiya* [one of the major daily Russian newspapers] reporter asked Hamas delegation leader Khalid Mashaal to comment on his June 2000 pronouncement that children should be trained as suicide bombers. The Hamas leader defended his comment. "We have our own symbols, our own examples to imitate. And we are proud of this," he told the assembled press. So what did Putin's outreach achieve? Again, Chechnya played front and center in his strategy: Hamas promised not to meddle in the North Caucasus.

What does the Hamas visit signal for Russian-Israeli relations? Under Putin, ties between Moscow and Jerusalem initially blossomed. The Russian president appreciated Jerusalem's no-nonsense approach to terrorism, as well as its technical assistance with regard to Chechnya. That one million Israelis speak Russian facilitates business. Economic relations between Moscow and Jerusalem thrived; hundreds of Israeli businesses operate in Russia. Russian business leaders look to fill Israel's growing energy needs. Today, direct trade between the two states is valued at approximately $1.5 billion. In April 2006, the Russian government launched an Israeli satellite capable of spying on the Iranian nuclear program. But while some writers once celebrated Putin's new approach, the enabling of Iran's nuclear program and the invitation to Hamas suggest that optimism regarding Russia's president is premature. While the Russian government is willing to criticize its Iranian and Arab clients to placate the West, it seldom translates harsh words into action. The Russian Foreign Ministry's contradictory statements following the July 12, 2006 Israeli incursion into southern Lebanon seemed designed to obfuscate rather than stake out a clear position against terror. The Russian government may appreciate the fruits of economic relations with Israel, but when it comes to standing on principle against terror, Putin draws a line. Russia does not consider Hamas or Hezbollah [a similar organization in Lebanon] to be terrorist groups; to stand too much with Israel against terror might mean undercutting Putin's Faustian bargain with Islamists over Chechnya.

Washington and Moscow Split in Middle East

The post-9-11 U.S.-Russian honeymoon did not last. While some tension resulted from Putin's growing authoritarianism, more responsible was Putin's decision to place Russia squarely in opposition to Washington's desire to contain Iranian nuclear ambitions, delegitimize terrorism, and promote democracy.

That Washington and Moscow diverge on the Middle East should not surprise. A June 2000 foreign policy concept paper approved by Putin defines Moscow's priorities in the Middle East "to restore and strengthen its position, particularly economic ones." Putin has pursued this strategic pragmatism even when it puts Moscow in the position of arming Iran and Syria while strengthening economic relations with Israel.

How wise is Putin's policy? Not all Russian analysts are convinced it will further Moscow's interests. Dmitri Suslov, an expert with Moscow's Council on Foreign and Defense Policy, explained, "[T]here is a big risk here, that by providing greater legitimacy for Islamists, Russia could invite greater instability in the Middle East and at home." Prominent Russian columnist Yulia Latynina argued that "by holding talks with rogue states, Russia comes perilously close to being perceived as a rogue state in its own right."

Nor is success assured for Putin's gamble that he can appease external Islamists to win space for Russian actions in Chechnya. In June 2006, Islamists in Iraq kidnapped and murdered four Russian diplomats—including one Muslim. They issued a tape declaring, *"God's verdict has been carried out on the Russian diplomats . . . in revenge for the torture, killing, and expulsion of our brothers and sisters by the infidel Russian government."* Simply put, Putin may subscribe to Realpolitik [politics of pragmatism rather than ideology], but Islamic extremists are not well-versed in its intricacies.

> *"Only a very small part of [Russian] society is getting richer. . . . The majority of the population lives in destitution."*

The Gap Between Rich and Poor Is Undermining Russian Society

Luke Harding

In the following viewpoint, Luke Harding describes the growing income gap in Russia as a serious problem: The vast majority of rural and urban Russians live under poorer conditions than they did in Soviet Russia, while rising oil and gas prices have made the government and a small class of industrialists very rich. Luke Harding is the Moscow correspondent for the Guardian, *a prominent British newspaper.*

As you read, consider the following questions:

1. What was Russia's foreign debt in 2007, and what does Harding estimate is Russia's current cash surplus?

2. Why do Kremlin economists argue against raising Russians' pensions, according to the author?

3. What was the income tax rate for Russia's lowest-income citizens in 2007, according to Harding? What was the income tax rate for Russia's wealthiest income bracket?

Standing in his fetid kitchen, Sasha Ivanovich shows off a bucket of muddy potatoes. Dug from his snow-encrusted garden, they are his lunch. In fact they are his supper too as, he points out, he has nothing else to eat.

"Everything has got more expensive. Bread has gone up. Cigarettes have gone up. My sister pays my gas bill. I can't afford vodka. Can you give me 100 roubles [about $4]?" he asks, hopefully.

Vast Wealth Is Not Trickling Down

Since Vladimir Putin took power [in 2000], Russia has enjoyed growing prosperity. The days when the country was forced to borrow billions from the IMF [International Monetary Fund], devalue the rouble, and beg for international help are a fading Yeltsin-era memory.

Instead, Russia has so much money that it doesn't know what to do with it. [In February 2007] President Putin boasted that the country had paid off its $22 [billion] foreign debt. Rising oil and gas prices have transformed its economic fortunes and made it a resurgent global force.

The Kremlin is now sitting on a vast mountain of cash, coyly known as the stabilisation fund. [In March 2007, it] topped $103.6 [billion]. (Others suggest Russia's total surplus is more like $300 [billion].) And the American magazine *Forbes* recently revealed that Russia has 53 billionaires, 20 more than [in 2006].

Unfortunately none of this has trickled down to Sasha, 56, who lives alone in a wooden cottage, and whose poor sight renders him unfit for work. Like many at the bottom of Russia's pile, Sasha survives not through the generosity of the state but thanks to his kindly neighbours.

His home, in the village of Lavrov, is a 45-minute drive from the town of Oryol in south-west Russia, past forests of silver birch. The young people have all left and most of the older men appear to have died—hardly surprising in a country where male life expectancy is 58. Like much of rural Russia, Lavrov appears to be on its last legs, along with many of its remaining citizens.

"It was much better during Soviet times," Tonya Fominyh, 79, says. "Pensions were small but equal. We lived well. Now our pensions are nothing."

Mrs Fominyh receives 1,540 roubles a month from the state. She spent three decades working for the Soviet police force but now survives on handouts from her son.

So far few of Russia's petro-billions [i.e., oil riches] have found their way to society's poorest groups: pensioners, the unemployed and government employees, including teachers and hospital workers. . . .

State Pensions Are Inadequate

Russia's orthodox church warned that the gulf between the rich and poor was growing wider, with some 20% of Russians below the poverty line. There is still no real middle-class and there is a significant gap between urban and rural life, the church said, warning: "Russia possesses between 30% and 40% of the earth's resources. Revenues from exports of natural resources built the stabilisation fund. But only a very small part of society is getting richer. It is doing so at a pace that amazes even some of the richest people in the world. On the other hand, the majority of the population lives in destitution."

It is not only pensioners in villages who are hard up. Sitting in her tiny flat in urban Oryol, Tatiana Tsherbakova gazes at a giant photo of a sun-kissed beach pasted to her living room wall. It is the Canaries, one of many places Mrs Tsherbakova, 68, would like to visit. "I don't have the money to

Up to 40 Percent of Russians Live in Poverty

Even a cursory examination of the social situation in modern Russia reveals a deeply divided society. An array of statistics documents the reality of two different worlds that hardly come into contact with one another. One—the world of wealth and luxury—is inhabited by an insignificant minority. The other—the world of social decline and an arduous struggle for life's necessities—is inhabited by millions upon millions.

Figures showing the distribution of wealth reveal the glaring nature of this social polarisation. According to government data, the incomes of the very richest members of Russian society are 15 times those of the poorest—one of the highest levels of social inequality to be found among the world's leading countries. In Moscow, this difference is 53-fold. . . .

Russia's National Statistics Office officially classifies a total of 31 million people (22 percent of the population) as poor. Other surveys, however, place the poverty rate at 40 percent or higher.

Vladimir Volkov and Julia Denenberg,
"Wealth and Poverty in Modern Russia,"
World Socialist Web Site, *March 11, 2005.*
www.wsws.org/articles/2005/mar2005/russ-m11.shtml.

travel," she explains. "It's my great passion. I've always wanted to see Vladivostok. But the train ticket is too expensive."

This is one of the strange ironies of post-Soviet Russia. Thirty years ago Mrs Tsherbakova was not allowed to travel to the west, but she took advantage of cheap internal fares to roam across the Soviet Union, holidaying in Moldova, swimming in the Black Sea and hiking in the Kazakh mountains. Now she is free to travel anywhere, but on her state pension of 5,600 roubles a month she cannot afford to.

Kremlin economists say they face a dilemma. It is impossible to raise pensions significantly, they argue, without increasing inflation, currently running at 9%. They also point out that Russia's 38 million pensioners claim their pensions much earlier than western Europeans—at 55 for women and 60 for men.

"I don't believe this [argument about inflation] to be true," said Natalia Rimashevskaya, a poverty expert at Moscow's Institute of Social and Economic Studies of Population. "At the moment 30% of all salaries are below the minimum needed to live. Pensions are very low. The average is 2,500 roubles. This leaves pensioners on the edge. If prices go up, they fall into poverty."

At his annual press conference [in February 2007] Mr Putin said that reducing social inequality would be one of his key tasks before he leaves office in 2008.

Average salaries have gone up significantly under Mr Putin. But the statistics conceal the fact that for millions, wages have hardly changed at all, Ms Rimashevskaya said. One of the biggest problems, she added, was the tax system, which saw [the wealthiest elite] oligarchs and road sweepers paying an identical tax rate of 13%.

Periodical Bibliography

The following articles have been selected to supplement the diverse views presented in this chapter.

Anna Arutunyan — "Medvedev Gets Tough on Corruption," *Moscow News*, May 22, 2008.

Fred Burton and Dan Burges — "Russian Organized Crime," *Strategic Forecasting*, November 14, 2007. www.stratfor.com/weekly/russian_organized_crime.

Jason Bush — "Big Shoes to Fill: Russia's Medvedev Gets Down to Business," *Spiegel Online*, May 9, 2008. www.spiegel.de/international/business/0,1518,552455,00.html.

Kommersant — "A New Generation of Russian Corruption," March 28, 2008. www.kommersant.com/p872353/bribery_corruption.

Clifford J. Levy — "At Expense of All Others, Putin Picks a Church," *New York Times*, April 24, 2008.

Guy Norton — "Infrastructure: Build Russia a Boom Before It Breaks Down," *Euromoney*, May 2008.

Renat Perelet, Serguey Pegov, and Mikhail Yulkin — "Climate Change: Russia Country Paper," *Human Development Report 2007/2008*, United Nations Development Programme, December 2007. http://hdr.undp.org/en/reports/global/hdr2007-2008/papers/perelet_renat_pegov_yulkin.pdf.

Nathan Thornburgh — "In Search of Russia's Big Idea," *Time*, December 20, 2008.

Shaun Walker — "Russian Town Is So Toxic Even the Mayor Wants It Closed Down," *Independent*, April 13, 2008.

For Further Discussion

Chapter 1: What Is Russia's Role in International Politics?

1. Fiona Hill supports her argument that Russia is the next energy superpower by describing its cooperative relationships with neighboring states, which represent a huge new market for Russian products, share common languages, and are Russia's biggest source of labor. Carol R. Saivetz, in contrast, cites political, economic, and cultural antagonism between Russia and neighboring states as reasons why Russia will *not* achieve superpower status. Which analysis do you think is more convincing? Use evidence from the viewpoints to support your answer.

2. Gary Hart argues that the United States needs Russia as a strategic partner for America's benefit (to fight terrorism, provide a stable oil supply, and influence Middle East politics in America's favor) and for the benefit of the world (to reduce nuclear arsenals and cooperatively fight global warming). John Edwards and Jack Kemp argue that an authentic partnership is all but impossible and the current tense relationship between Russia and the United States is likely to get worse. Based on evidence from the viewpoints, do you believe the costs of *not* working together outweigh the real differences and lingering antagonisms between the two countries?

3. Ed Blanche and Peter Zeihan debate Russia's present and future political and economic influence in various parts of the world, compared both to Russia's past influence and to current U.S. influence in regions such as the Middle East. Based on their arguments, do you think global political

stability depends on a country's alliance with either Russia or the United States? If you believe future alliances are critical, where does Russia have vital interests?

4. Matthew Bunn and Anthony Wier say Russia has made substantial progress in locking down its nuclear arsenal and civilian nuclear facilities, conceding some vulnerability to theft and terrorism. The National Intelligence Council argues that these vulnerabilities are dangerously, unacceptably high. Based on their arguments, how secure is "secure enough" in the debate over nuclear stockpiles?

Chapter 2: Is Russia Moving Toward Democracy?

1. Based on Vyacheslav Nikonov's comparison of the Russian and U.S. political systems and Peter Wilson's comparison of Russian and U.S. elections, why do you agree or disagree with Nikonov's assertion that a government does not need separation of powers to be democratic?

2. Orlando Figes and Stephen Kotkin both focus on Russian popular attitudes—apathy, a long historical tradition of paternalism, love of country—in debating Russia's movement toward or away from democracy. In which direction are these attitudes likely to influence Russian politics, in your view?

3. Russian president Dmitry Medvedev vowed to uphold Russians' constitutional rights in his 2008 inaugural address, and the Kremlin has denied involvement in recent highly publicized poisonings and murders of political dissidents. Michael Specter points to laws that permit the assassination of "enemies of the Russian regime" as violations of the Russian constitution and an indication that the Kremlin is prepared to act outside the law, even if its denials of involvement in specific cases are true. Which accusations of state-sponsored violence described in the viewpoints are based on factual evidence and which are based on unfounded speculation, in your view?

Chapter 3: How Is Western Culture Influencing Russia?

1. Steve Liesman sees the Russian consumer bubble as a good thing, based on rising standards of living. Yasha Levine sees the Russian consumer bubble as a bad thing, based on rising debt levels. Which argument do you find more persuasive, and why?

2. Viv Groskop highlights the significant influence of Western culture on the growing elite class in Russian society, while Fred Weir discusses steps the Russian government is taking to strengthen its Eastern heritage. Based on the authors' arguments, do you think this duality between Western and Eastern lifestyles can be resolved? Why or why not?

3. Olga Sharapova is a journalist specializing in travel, arts, and cultural subjects. Irina Ivakhnyuk is a professor of economics specializing in transit migration issues. In what ways might their professional expertise and backgrounds bias their views on Western migration to Russia and Russian migration to the West? Which author makes the stronger case, in your view, and why?

Chapter 4: What Is Russia's Greatest Challenge?

1. There are two ways to counter Russian depopulation: from within, by stimulating the birth rate, reducing the infant mortality rate, and improving public health and living standards to raise life expectancy; and from without, by increasing immigration and slowing emigration. According to Victor Yasmann, Russia is committed to increasing its population from within. Luke Harding argues that Russia's young people will keep leaving as long as the gulf between the rich and the poor keeps growing. How do you believe demographic change is best achieved in Russia, based on arguments in Yasmann's and Harding's viewpoints?

2. How do Russian environmental problems affect public health, transportation networks, water supplies, and national security *outside* as well as within Russia, according to Mark A. Smith?

3. Moisés Naím criticizes Nigeria and Venezuela as oil-rich "petro-states," plagued by weak democratic institutions, a poorly functioning public sector, and a high concentration of power and wealth. He praises Norway as an oil-rich country that is *not* a petro-state because it has a strong democracy and an effective public sector. Unless democracy is strengthened in Russia, he warns, it is doomed to political conflict and economic decline. In your view, are Naím's parameters valid predictors of Russia's future stability and success, and can they be applied not just to Russia but to major oil-producing countries around the world? Why or why not?

Organizations to Contact

The editors have compiled the following list of organizations concerned with the issues debated in this book. The descriptions are derived from materials provided by the organizations. All have publications or information available for interested readers. The list was compiled on the date of publication of the present volume; street and online addresses may change. Be aware that many organizations take several weeks or longer to respond to inquiries, so allow as much time as possible.

American Enterprise Institute (AEI)
1150 17th St. NW, Washington, DC 20036
(202) 862-5800 • fax: (202) 862-7177
Web site: www.aei.org

The American Enterprise Institute for Public Policy Research is an independent, nonprofit research organization associated with the neoconservative movement in American foreign policy and Republican administrations since the 1980s. The Web site offers an archive of op-eds, newsletters, and short papers such as "Putinism" and "Why Russia Holds 'Elections.'" AEI publishes the quarterly *Russian Outlook*, which examines key social, political, and economic trends from a conservative perspective.

Brookings Institution
1775 Massachusetts Ave. NW, Washington, DC 20036
(202) 797-6000
e-mail: brookinfo@brookings.edu
Web site: www.brookings.org

The Brookings Institution, founded in 1927, is a liberal-centrist think tank whose fellows conduct research on and debate issues of foreign policy, economics, government, and the social sciences. Its scholars publish analyses of U.S.-Russia relations in the quarterly journal *Brookings Review* and in position papers such as "Putin's Plan: The Future of 'Russia Inc.'" and "Russia Resurgent: The Once and Future Superpower," which examines what Russia's re-emergence as a global force means for arms control.

Embassy of the Russian Federation

2650 Wisconsin Ave. NW, Washington, DC   20007
(202) 298-5700 • fax: (202) 298-5735
Web site: www.russianembassy.org

The Russian embassy is the official delegation of the Russian government in the United States, headed since 1999 by ambassador Yuri V. Ushakov. Besides facilitating official functions such as processing visa and adoption applications, the embassy Web site provides a wide range of information useful to student researchers: links profile Russian geography, culture, and government structure; the history of Russian-American relations including trade agreements, summit meetings, and an updated archive of news articles; and English translations of Russian legislative proceedings, press reports, and political speeches.

Foreign Policy Research Institute

1528 Walnut St., Suite 610, Philadelphia, PA   19102
(215) 732-3774 • fax: (215) 732-4401
e-mail: fpri@fpri.org
Web site: www.fpri.org

Founded in 1955, the Foreign Policy Research Institute conducts research on both pressing issues and long-term questions: the war on terrorism, relations with Russia, the roles of religion, and ethnicity in international politics, among others. It advises policy makers, scholars, and the general public in the effort to develop policies that advance the national interest. It publishes its findings in a quarterly journal, *Orbis* and a bulletin series for teachers called *Footnotes* via e-mail and the Web site. Recent relevant articles include "Russkiy and Rossiiskiy: Russian National Identity After Putin."

Heritage Foundation
214 Massachusetts Ave. NE, Washington, DC   20002
(202) 546-4400 • fax: (202) 546-0904
e-mail: info@heritage.org
Web site: www.heritage.org

The Heritage Foundation is a conservative public policy research institute dedicated to "principles of free enterprise, limited government, individual freedom, traditional American values, and a strong national defense." Its resident scholars publish position papers on a wide range of complex issues in its *Backgrounder* series and in its quarterly journal *Policy Review*.

Hoover Institution
434 Galvez Mall, Stanford, CA   94305-6010
(650) 723-1754 • fax: (650) 723-1687
Web site: www.hoover.org

The Hoover Institution is a public policy research center devoted to advanced study of political economy and international affairs. It publishes the quarterly journal *Hoover Digest*, which occasionally includes articles on Russia, as well as a newsletter and reports. Of particular interest is a special 2008 online research project, "The Russian Economy" (www.hoover.org/research/russianecon), which puts Russian economic growth and contraction in global perspective with the help of maps and charts. This site clearly explains Russia's transition from a centrally planned socialist economy in the Soviet era to a market economy today, with helpful supplemental charts and maps.

ITAR-TASS News Agency
10-12, Tverskoy Blvd., Moscow, Russia   125993
+7 (495) 629-7925
e-mail: info@itar-tass.com
Web site: www.itar-tass.com/eng

In existence since 1904, the ITAR-TASS News Agency (successor to the Soviet TASS) is Russia's state central information agency and one of the world's largest news organizations, with more than 130 bureaus in Russia and abroad. In addition to round-the-clock news in full English translation, the Web site (ITAR-TASS Online link) offers an electronic data bank containing all agency materials produced since 1987, multimedia products, and updated reference e-books on Russia and other CIS member states. The organization is both a valuable source of information on day-to-day Russian affairs and, as TASS is state-funded, useful to students in comparisons of independent and state-sponsored media.

Kennan Institute
One Woodrow Wilson Plaza, 1300 Pennsylvania Ave. NW
Washington, DC   20004
(202) 691-4100
e-mail: kennan@wilsoncenter.org
Web site: www.wilsoncenter.org/kennan

The Kennan Institute is the oldest program of the Woodrow Wilson Center, a nonpartisan public affairs research center. The institute is committed to improving American expertise about Russia and other successor states to the Soviet Union. It organizes seminars, briefings, and conferences drawing on prominent scholars and policy makers with experience in shaping U.S.-Russia policy. It also funds research projects in the humanities and social sciences relating to Russia, Ukraine, and other former Soviet states. Books, briefs, and reports available on the Web site include "Moscow and Kyiv: Changing Cities and Migrant Magnets" and "Religion in Russian Society: State Policy, Regional Challenges, and Individual Rights."

Russian Cultural Centre
1825 Phelps Pl. NW, Washington, DC   20008
(202) 265-3840 • fax: (202) 265-6040
e-mail: rcc@rccusa.org
Web site: www.rccusa.org

The Russian Cultural Centre, founded in 1997, is a bilateral project of the Russian Ministry of Foreign Affairs and the U.S. State Department. The center is dedicated to developing and maintaining positive relations between the Russian and American people by sponsoring activities and offering information related to Russian education, the arts, commerce, athletics, and science. Web site resources available in English include news archives, a calendar of cultural events, a catalog of audio books, and links to Russian-American clubs across the United States.

U.S. Department of State

2201 C St. NW, Washington, DC   20520
(202) 647-4000
Web site: www.state.gov/p/eur/

The State Department's Bureau of European and Eurasian Affairs is the federal bureau directly concerned with U.S.-Russia relations and diplomacy. Daily news updates about current events are posted on the Web site. In addition to country background notes with statistical information on Russian geography, demographics, and government, the Web site also offers fact sheets, maps, quick links to major reports, the timeline "200 Years of U.S.-Russia Relations," and the text of speeches, congressional testimony, and official agreements.

Bibliography of Books

Leon Aron   *Russia's Revolution: 1989–2006.* Washington, DC: AEI, 2007.

Zoltan Barany   *Democratic Breakdown and the Decline of the Russian Military.* Princeton, NJ: Princeton University Press, 2007.

Andrew Barnes   *Owning Russia: The Struggle over Factories, Farms, and Power.* Ithaca, NY: Cornell University Press, 2006.

Birgit Beumers   *Pop Culture Russia!: Media, Arts, and Lifestyle.* Santa Barbara, CA: ABC-CLIO, 2005.

Douglas Blum, ed.   *Russia and Globalization: Identity, Security, and Society in an Era of Change.* Baltimore, MD: Johns Hopkins University Press, 2008.

Eliot Borenstein   *Overkill: Sex and Violence in Contemporary Russian Pop Culture.* Ithaca, NY: Cornell University Press, 2007.

Melissa L. Caldwell   *Not by Bread Alone: Social Support in the New Russia.* Berkeley: University of California Press, 2004.

John T. Connor   *Out of the Red: Investment and Capitalism in Russia.* New York: Wiley, 2008.

Padma Desai   *Conversations on Russia: Reform from Yeltsin to Putin.* New York: Oxford University Press, 2006.

Stephen Fortescue *Russia's Oil Barons and Metal Magnates: Oligarchs and the State in Transition*. New York: Palgrave Macmillan, 2007.

Clifford G. Gaddy *Russia's Addiction: The Political*
and Barry *Economy of Resource Dependence.*
William Ickes Washington, DC: Brookings Institution Press, 2008.

John Giduck *Terror at Beslan: A Russian Tragedy with Lessons for America's Schools.* Golden, CO: Archangel Group, 2005.

Marshall I. *Petrostate: Putin, Power, and the New*
Goldman *Russia*. New York: Oxford University Press, 2008.

———— *The Piratization of Russia: Russian Reform Goes Awry*. New York: Routledge, 2003.

Loren R. Graham *Science in the New Russia*. Blooming-
and Irina Dezhina ton: Indiana University Press, 2008.

David Hoffman *The Oligarchs: Wealth and Power in the New Russia*. New York: Public Affairs, 2003.

Sharon Hudgins *The Other Side of Russia: A Slice of Life in Siberia and the Russian Far East*. College Station: Texas A&M University Press, 2004.

James Hughes *Chechnya: From Nationalism to Jihad*. Philadelphia: University of Pennsylvania Press, 2007.

Zoe Knox | *Russian Society and the Orthodox Church: Religion in Russia After Communism*. London: Routledge, 2004.

Alena V. Ledeneva | *How Russia Really Works: The Informal Practices That Shaped Post-Soviet Politics and Business*. Ithaca, NY: Cornell University Press, 2006.

Edward Lucas | *The New Cold War: Putin's Russia and the Threat to the West*. New York: Palgrave Macmillan, 2008.

John Mole | *I Was a Potato Oligarch: Travels and Travails in the New Russia*. London: Nicholas Brealey, 2008.

Paul Murphy | *The Wolves of Islam: Russia and the Faces of Chechen Terror*. Dulles, VA: Potomac, 2006.

Joel M. Ostrow | *The Consolidation of Dictatorship in Russia: An Inside View of the Demise of Democracy*. Westport, CT: Praeger, 2007.

Anna Politkovskaya | *Putin's Russia: Life in a Failing Democracy*. Translated by Arch Tait. New York: Henry Holt, 2004.

——— | *A Russian Diary: A Journalist's Final Account of Life, Corruption, and Death in Putin's Russia*. New York: Random House, 2007.

William Pridemore | *Ruling Russia: Law, Crime, and Justice in a Changing Society*. Lanham, MD: Rowman & Littlefield, 2007.

Steven Rosefielde — *Russia in the 21st Century: The Prodigal Superpower.* Cambridge, England: Cambridge University Press, 2004.

Joseph D. Serio — *Investigating the Russian Mafia.* Durham, NC: Carolina Academic Press, 2008.

Lilia Shevtsova — *Russia: Lost in Translation.* Translated by Arch Tait. Washington, DC: Carnegie Endowment for International Peace, 2007.

Michael Stuermer — *Putin and the Rise of Russia: The Country That Came In from the Cold.* London: George Weidenfeld & Nicholson, 2008.

Dmitri V. Trenin — *Getting Russia Right.* Washington, DC: Carnegie Endowment for International Peace, 2007.

David White — *The Russian Democratic Party Yabloko: Opposition in a Managed Democracy.* Hampshire, UK: Ashgate, 2006.

Andrew Wilson — *Virtual Politics: Faking Democracy in the Post-Soviet World.* New Haven, CT: Yale University Press, 2005.

Index